Choose Success - Ignite the Power Within

Feeling stuck? Activate your power of choice; discover and use the proven 5-step Conscious Transformation Process to create the outcomes you desire and deserve.

Patricia Altvater, M.A.

To order contact:
Transformations Institute
6062 Wood Dr.
Waterville, OH 43566
877-211-9534

Acknowledgments

There are many people I'd like to thank for encouraging and helping me during the journey which culminated with this book -- Choose Success – Ignite the Power Within.

I truly appreciate:

➤ *Fred for his constant support and love*

➤ *Rebecca Booth, Marketing Goddess, for the wonderful work she did on the illustrations and layout of this book.*

➤ *Rebecca Taylor for being a fantastic accomplice*

➤ *My clients that allowed their stories to be shared in this book*

➤ *The many people who attended my workshops and graciously took the time to write and tell me how the information changed their lives*

Table of Contents

Create Your Life on YOUR Terms

Chapter 1
You Have the Power

You can **ignite your inner power** and be a co-creator of your life. Don't worry, you don't need matches. This book will give you the tools to choose success - to choose to BE successful now and ultimately attain the outcomes you desire. It's about using your ability to choose and attract what you want, after releasing sabotaging mindsets and limiting core beliefs; it doesn't matter how you define success. It could be wealth, love, wellness, a thriving business, optimal health, peace, happiness, or empowering relationships.

The principles to attract from your inner power, that you are going to learn in this book, will help you deliberately create your life. You'll learn to BE successful, to really feel that way, even before you've achieved the outcomes you desire. Afterall, true success has nothing to do with the outcome you are after; it has to do with how you feel along the way.

We live in a society where many people never activate their power of choice; to consciously choose their beliefs, thoughts and emotions. I've noticed individuals that repeat the same self-destructive behavior patterns over and over in their lives. To be

honest, I've done that a few times myself. Why do we do that? Are we just slow learners? Sometimes we are! We are oblivious to the subconscious belief that's driving the experience and until we become aware of and change the belief, we just keep repeating these self-defeating patterns over and over. Sometimes we engage different players to keep our lives interesting but the belief remains waiting for us to recognize and transform it.

Some people don't want to change; they prefer to remain victims, living in the basement of their lives, as Iyanla Vanzant so aptly describes it in her wonderful book *In the Meantime; Finding Yourself and the Love You Want*. I'm sure you know a few victims; they are the people that when you see them after a 6 month or more hiatus, still have the same story line going on in their life and darn it, if they don't want to share those all too familiar details with you. Run for your life! Don't fall into your own basement.

Become a Co-creator

As a co-creator, you leave victim mentality behind because your life is no longer dictated by circumstance. Co-creation simply means shaping a new reality by partnering with the divine flow, rather than trying to control it. If you are a control freak like me, you know that's easier said than done! However, once you experience it, you'll never go back to forcing your preferred outcomes. When you use the power within to transform your life and experience success, you'll discover that the results are so much more than you ever dreamed possible.

To demonstrate what I mean, let me tell you about Tim. When he arrived in my office, he was at the breaking point financially after pouring all his resources, over the last four years, into a start-up business. When we discussed the **essence** of what he considered success regarding his career, this is the list he created:

1. freedom of time
2. decision making ability
3. unlimited earnings potential
4. lead a team of people
5. mentally stimulating work
6. purposeful work

Tim mentally created a prototype, from this list, of what he considered career success. At first, he thought success meant having his own business; he doubted he could obtain a job in the challenged economy, especially since he was in his late 50's. However, through coaching he realized that all he had to do was get to the essence of what he wanted and then stay open to any and all opportunities that came his way. Guess what happened?? He got a six figure/ year job that met all of his criteria within two weeks!

He co-created his new reality by getting clear about what he wanted and **believing** it would happen. Tim said, "Shortly after our session, I had this thought that I should look on the Internet for jobs. Somehow I found this site that specialized in job openings in my field and before I knew it, I had three interviews and landed this perfect job!"

You can co-create what you want; you'll learn to use the Conscious Transformation Process™ described in the upcoming chapters to manifest your desires, just like Tim did. Holding this book means you are ready to embrace, or already do, the concept that you truly are the co-creator of your life. Your thoughts create your reality and you choose your thoughts. I know, sometimes it feels like they choose you! The Conscious Transformation Process™ will help you deliberately create your life and transform sabotaging beliefs, like Tim's belief about his age and the economy. This will improve your chances for successfully making important changes and **igniting your inner power.**

You can choose success and deliberately create whatever you desire by following the five step Conscious Transformation Process™ of 1.) Announce, 2.) Align, 3.) Act, 4.) Account and 5.) Allow. In the following chapters, you'll first learn about limiting mindsets that can hamper your ability to consciously create the life you desire. Then you will learn how to apply the Conscious Transformation Process™ in your life.

Enjoy The Journey

Life is about the NOW and not the destination you seek, so relax and feel good today, knowing that you will be successful at this technique. The Conscious Transformations Process™ is not about fixing you; you are perfect the way you are! More than anything, this process is about honoring and loving yourself, while increasing awareness of and then releasing limiting beliefs and mindsets. Once this transformation is accomplished, you can go on to expand your capacity to create and to love, both yourself and others. This in itself will bring your life much joy.

Chapter 2
Everything Is Energy

Do you know that you are able to actually transform your body's biology with your mind? How powerful is that! A friend of mine was diagnosed with a rare and highly aggressive cancer, a Sinonasal Undifferentiated Carcinoma (SNUC), in March 2006. By October 2006, his cancer was totally gone; his doctors called it a miracle. His treatment included all of the doctor's recommendations, which for most SNUC patients is not enough. He also included many body/mind activities such as visualization, affirmations and complete belief that he was one of the 5% that typically survive this type of cancer. He survived!

Too often we use the power of our mind to create emotional havoc within ourselves pertaining to the realization of our dreams. We say we want one thing, but don't believe it's really possible to achieve that particular thing. Using the five step Conscious Transformation Process™, you will learn to harness the power of your mind to create your ideal life.

All of Creation Is Energy

Quantum physicists have discovered that anything and everything that exists is a vibrating frequency of pure energy. That means that any particular item that you can name – a tree, a car, a house, a desk, a physical body, a thought, a feeling, everything, has at its core the same vibrating pure energy. Doesn't that just blow your mind? I had a hard time accepting that my refrigerator is actually made up of the same energy as I am. However, it's proven by scientists and I'm now convinced that they are right.

We use the word energy in different contexts. Such as, the energy that powers the electricity in a home, the energy that fuels a car and gives it the ability to move, and the energy that is felt within a body. Although these types of energy seem different, when analyzed to the smallest sub-atomic particle, they are at their core made up of the same vibrating frequency of energy. It is this one energy that makes up all things, which means we really are all connected and all one, just as the most enlightened spiritual teachers of the past have proclaimed.

Einstein was the first scientist to discover that energy is at the core of everything; he believed that this energy took the form of solid particles. Thomas Young, another physicist working during the time of Einstein, agreed that energy was at the core sub-atomic level. However, he believed that the energy was not solid, but waves. It turns out they were both correct. It was later proven by The Copenhagen Interpretation that the thoughts and perceptions (beliefs) of the scientist doing the observation is what determines whether the energy appears as a wave or a particle.

That's about as deep into science as I am going to take you; let's now examine how this discovery impacts your ability to be the creator of your life experience. If you want to know more about the science behind the concepts, review the section called References and Suggesed Reading in the back of this book.

In this chapter, we discovered that quantum energy acts and responds consistently with the thoughts and beliefs of the scientist studying it. This implies that everything exists as a wave which then through observation and expectation is transformed into a physical form based upon the thoughts and beliefs of the individual observing. In other words, your thoughts and beliefs create your reality.

Quantum physics and conventional religion both support this theory. When consciously applying these principles, you will experience how your beliefs and thinking create matter and how famous Bible quotes, such as, "All things whatsoever thou wilt, believe thou hast received, and thou shall receive." apply to manifesting a healthy, happy, prosperous life!

Contrary to what you may have believed in the past, you truly do not have to be a victim in your life. Really! You have the ability to create your reality based on how you choose to think, believe and feel. Your thoughts and feelings about them (pure energy) are broadcast outward into the infinite field of wave energy and then join together with other additional energies that are of the same

frequecy. Collectively, these energies, based upon your expectations, join to shape what you see and experience in form, in your physical reality. Whatever you think about and truly believe, even if there's no basis for that belief, determines how your life unfolds. Beth's story will help you understand.

My friend, Beth was stressed. She'd traveled to Boulder, Colorado from her home in New York for what she thought would be a weekend visit to check in on her mother. Upon arriving, she realized her mother's health was much worse than expected and knew she needed to make plans to stay all summer.

Beth found a temporary place to live for a few weeks and decided to use the principles we've just been discussing to locate a home that would allow her to release her worries about her living arrangement and focus instead on helping her mother recover. Each morning, before she got out of bed, Beth visualized her ideal house: comfortable, filled with healing energy, and, importantly, located close to her mother. She believed that it was possible to find this ideal house. She also took action toward her goal by telling as many people as possible about her situation.

Shortly thereafter, Beth received a call from a woman she didn't know. Terry was a friend of a friend who'd heard Beth was looking for a place to stay and wondered if she'd be interested in house sitting for Terry's parents. Beth smiled when she discovered, in this town of 100,000 people, the beautiful home was located just two blocks from her mother's retirement community. As an added bonus, the word "JOY" was posted prominently throughout the home – placed there by Terry's mother who was, appropriately, named Joy.

Beth spent the summer in Terry's parents' home, "surrounded by Joy" (as she puts it) and well-equipped to give her mother the care she needed. Since then, Beth's mother's health has improved and Beth manifested another home four blocks away from her mother with a guest room where Beth can stay anytime, for as long as she wants. Beth says this experience has deepened her relationship with her mother and led to the creation of several new friendships.

Life works like this because when your thoughts and emotions intersect, feelings are created, which according to quantum physics, create vibrations. The unlimited field of possibility, just like a magnet, matches whatever you are offering in terms of vibration returning to you more of what you are giving out. Beth obviously created a strong, clear vibration concerning finding her perfect home away from home.

In *The Biology of Belief*, author Dr. Bruce Lipton, a former medical school professor and research scientist, examines in great detail the processes by which cells receive information and further explains how our thoughts and feelings create our personal experience. He has proven that genes and DNA do not control our biology; that instead DNA is controlled by signals from outside the cell, including the energetic messages emanating from our empowering and disempowering thoughts. His research explains why and how my friend cured his cancer.

During an interview, Dr. Lipton discussed a research study where Japanese children, allergic to a poison ivy-like plant, took part in an experiment. A leaf from the poisonous plant was rubbed on one forearm and a non-poisonous leaf, that looked similar to the poisonous leaf, was rubbed on the other forearm. The children were told which arm was exposed to which leaf and as expected, the children all broke out with a rash on the arm rubbed with the toxic leaf.

What the kids didn't know was that the leaves were purposely mislabeled. They broke out from the non-toxic leaf! In the majority of cases, no rash resulted from contact with the toxic leaf. That shows the power of our beliefs!

Summary

Penny Pierce, the author of *frequency – the Power of Personal Vibration,* expresses the true importance of energy to co-creation:

".... *your personal vibration – the frequency of energy you hold moment by moment in your body, emotions and mind – is the most important tool you have for creating and living your ideal life. If your energy frequency is high, fast, and clear, life unfolds effortlessly and in alignment with your destiny, while a lower, slower, more distorted frequency begets a life of snags and disappointments."*

www.transformationsinstitute.com

Mischievous Mindsets

Chapter 3
What Is Your Mindset Telling You?

Have you noticed "Your thoughts create your reality." is one of my favorite expressions? However, it's not totally correct because your thoughts are not the point of origin. Thoughts arise from core beliefs which are framed by mindsets.

The continuum is core beliefs create mindsets which give rise to thoughts. Our thoughts then result in emotions which energetically effect our actions and ignite the vibrations that move us on our path. So it looks like this:

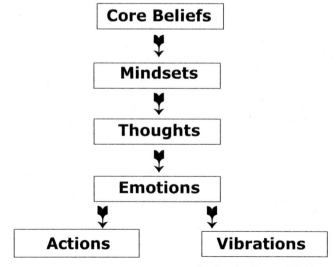

EMPOWERING

thoughts

invite

HIGH

vibrations!

woohoo!

The psychological treatment called Cognitive Behavior Therapy is a variation of this concept. The purpose of this therapy is to transform emotions and actions by changing thoughts and beliefs. It is not about providing rationalizations or intellectual excuses for things but rather it's about examining your thoughts, emotions and actions to see if at the deepest level the beliefs are distorted in some way. Which they generally are when there are disempowering feelings involved.

How do we view this same concept on a metaphysical level? As I mentioned earlier, the vibrations emitted based upon your feelings, act like big magnets and attract, draw, or pull towards you the people, events, opportunities, etc. that are a "vibrational match" to the vibrations you are emitting.

So if we give attention to a situation that feels good, we give off high energy clear vibrations and attract more situations that are favorable. If we give attention to a situation that doesn't feel good – one which makes us feel angry, fearful, upset, worried, or disappointed - then we emit low energy feeling vibrations. They attract more unfavorable situations into our lives.

The quality of our life is a direct reflection of the core beliefs and mindsets that we hold. The beliefs and mindsets are typically at the subconscious level, so most of us are not even aware of the forces that are driving us to think, do or say what we do. If these inner most beliefs are not consistent with what we want to BE, DO or HAVE, then it is impossible to achieve our goals and dreams.

However, there is hope because awareness is the first step and beliefs and mindsets can be changed!

Core Beliefs

A belief is a conviction of the truth that was passed on to you by people you respected, so you have no reason to doubt it's validity. It is something that you believe as true and can be either conscious or unconscious. Beliefs are typically formed in childhood and may have helped you cope with your life at that time.

It's a limiting belief if it makes you feel unhappy, disappointed, sad or any other low energy feeling. An empowering belief, on the other hand, results in high level vibrational feelings and beneficial actions. We attract events that support our beliefs and even make the evidence of a circumstance fit our belief through our mindsets.

Pam had been married for nine years. She and her husband were happy with two children and a middle class life. However, Pam subconsciously held the belief that she was not lovable and would, therefore, be rejected at some point. As a result of her beliefs, she acted out in ways that her husband couldn't understand. She always sabotaged his efforts to go on fishing trips with his buddies or constantly questioned him about where he was and what he was doing when he wasn't with her, especially when she traveled out of town for business. On a conscious level, Pam didn't really understand why she acted like she did but rationalized that if her husband didn't want to spend all of his time with her and the kids, then he must not love them.

So guess what happened? Right – he had an affair! Her subconscious beliefs worked to create the reality that she feared and the perfect Universal energy field picked up on her fear and delivered to her exactly what she was vibrating. Was Pam totally the cause of the state of affairs (no pun intended!) of her marriage? No, of course not! However, she probably actually attracted a man to marry that had tendencies to cheat because of her underlying fear based beliefs.

How wonderful for her that she obtained the counseling that she needed to see her part in the events that occurred and didn't just blame her husband. So instead of ending up bitter and unhappy, she took the opportunity to learn and grow from the situation. Her husband also worked on himself and his beliefs and values. As a result, she and her husband reconciled and are creating a totally different relationship based on their new understandings.

The following chart is just a sampling of core beliefs:

Limiting Belief	Empowering Belief
You have to work hard for money	The world is abundant, there's enough for all
I don't deserve	I deserve all life has to offer
I'm not enough	I am enough just as I am
I'm not lovable	I am lovable
Life is a struggle	Life flows easily

"Flick"

We can change our
thoughts in an
instant

Mindsets

A mindset is defined as a habitual or characteristic mental attitude that determines how you interpret and respond to situations. Another definition calls it a frame of reference or perception. Mindsets come before thoughts on the continuum since they provide the framework or give us a way to interpret conditions. They are basically our views about the events, relationships and situations in our life based upon the core beliefs that we hold.

Have you heard the saying "perception equals reality"? Do you believe it? I do! The same experience can happen to several people and each person may have a different thought and emotion about it based on their mindset. For example, I offer retreats for women twice a year and one year the retreat was scheduled about a month before my daughter was expected to deliver twins. What if something had happened to her and I needed to cancel the retreat at the last minute. Some of the participants might have been angry, some disappointed and some might have thought – cool, twins!! It's the same event, but each person's mindset gives rise to their thoughts and feelings.

Saying "I can't help the way I feel" makes you a victim of misery and ultimately, you're just fooling yourself, because you can change how you feel. You can change your mindset so that your experience of external events does not cause you unhappiness.

Thoughts

Thoughts occur from the process of thinking or logically reasoning. Our thoughts arise from a mental activity and we have CONTROL over our mind; WE CAN change our mind in an instant!

You can learn to change the way you think, feel and act, right now. That simple but revolutionary principle can change your life. The thought messages you give yourself affect your emotions, so by learning to change your thoughts, you can change the way you feel.

What you will learn, when you work through the Transformations Breakthrough Process™ in Appendix A, is that most of the harmful thoughts you hold, which create low vibrational feelings, are distorted and unrealistic and stem from core beliefs that are not valid. We often fool ourselves and create internal and external misery by telling ourselves things that simply aren't true and sadly, we have no clue that we are the ones creating this havoc in our own lives.

Emotions

Emotions are energy in motion. Candace Pert's very interesting book called *The Molecules of Emotion* reveals that emotions are in all of our cells. That makes sense because if emotions are energy and our energy comes from our cells, then emotions must be in every cell. The feelings that are generated from our emotions are often accompanied by physiological changes, such as the knot in our stomach that happens the minute we see the police car pull out of its hiding spot and start to tail us.

Gregg Braden, in his powerful book, *The Spontaneous Healing of Belief,* says that there are really just two emotions - love and it's opposite, which

I will call fear. When our thoughts connect with the emotions of either love or fear, powerful feelings are created. We create feelings which then fuel our actions, such as the flight or fight response that is inherent in our bodies. Sometimes our feelings move us forward and sometimes they don't.

Bev was afraid to make her annual doctors appointment. She was already three months past the anniversary date and she just couldn't get herself to make the call to schedule the visit. Her fear and a feeling she couldn't quite pinpoint were keeping her paralyzed.

When I started questioning her about this, my first goal was to get to the thought behind the fear. It turns out Bev thought the doctor would be unhappy with her and reprimand her because she had gained weight since her last appointment. Bev had gained about ten pounds and so she was now a size 14 instead of the 12 she had been the year before. She was so afraid that the doctor would tell her she had to lose weight that she couldn't even set the appointment.

As we worked through the questions in the Transformations Breakthrough Process™ (Appendix A) here is how our conversation went:

> Pat: "Why would that (having the doctor mention her weight to her) cause the emotion of FEAR?"
>
> Bev: "I don't want someone commenting about my weight."
>
> Pat: "Why?"
>
> Bev: "Because it makes me feel bad."
>
> Pat: "Other than bad, identify another feeling

that comes up when someone comments on your weight. What would that be?"

Bev: "Disgusted – I don't want to be judged – I know I need to lose weight. I'm disgusted that I haven't been able to motivate myself to do it."

Pat: "Why would you think the doctor is judging you, when it's her job to help you be a healthy person?"

Bev: "I don't like to place myself in situations where people may say something about my weight because I've been judged before and I didn't like it, it made me feel inadequate."

Pat: "Is there more to this?"

Bev: "Now I remember, when I was a kid, my Dad said to me "You're not as thin as you think you are." That comment made me feel unworthy."

Bev was experiencing a perfectionist mindset created by the limiting belief that people judge you based on how you look and if you want to please them and receive their love, you need to look a certain way. Of course, her thoughts were distorted because doctors are trained to give advice, a doctor probably wouldn't mention weight to someone with only ten pounds to lose, and her Dad's comment was probably a flip remark which was certainly not intended to create a lifetime of insecurity. Her Dad probably doesn't even remember the incident.

Basically, the core belief Bev held of "I'm not enough as I am" resulted in a perfectionist mindset that framed everything based upon the perception that if you aren't perfect, people will make comments or degrade you and then you'll feel humiliated and embarrassed. That mindset caused thoughts such as

Bev's "I don't want to go to my doctor's appointment because I've gained weight." Her mindset and core belief were subconscious; she didn't realize the deeper reasons why she didn't want to go to the doctor. Her feelings of anxiety and worry resulted in the action of postponing the call to schedule the appointment. Working through this process gave Bev awareness; the first step in the Transformations Breakthrough Process™.

So as you can see from Bev's example, beliefs, mindsets and emotions create the feelings that are the driving force behind your actions or lack thereof. They can either help you, if they are empowering, or hinder you if they are limiting.

In the next three chapters you will learn more about three limiting mindsets that I've seen hold my clients back from achieving their desires. There are many variations of mindsets but I believe the most pervasive are these three:

1.   The Perfectionist Mindset

2.   The Instant Gratification Mindset

3.   The Scarcity Mindset

We'll examine these mindsets together in the next three chapters, so you can see if they apply to you. The core beliefs behind the mindsets are typically the limiting beliefs mentioned earlier in this chapter, such as "I am not enough", "I don't deserve" or "I am not lovable" You can use the Transformations Breakthrough Process™ in Appendix A to uncover yours and release them. You can not create the life of your dreams or manifest what you want while operating from limiting mindsets and core beliefs.

Remember, this is not about fixing you. You are fine exactly how you are; it's your birth right. This is actually about releasing your core beliefs that you ARE NOT fine just as you are! Those beliefs are distorted. These distortions manifest as mindsets which are easy to relate to; you may see yourself in the chapters that follow and be able to use those mindset examples to find your limiting core beliefs quickly.

I don't mean to imply that it's easy to change because it isn't; it requires dedication to the process. But it can be done and the result is worth it. You'll be able to use the step by step Conscious Transformation Process™ described later in this book to **ignite the power within** and manifest everything you want for your life.

Chapter 4
The Perfectionist Mindset

It's difficult to ignite the power within if you are living the life of a perfectionist. I know; I spent many years attempting to live up to unrealistic standards. Do you identify with any of these?

Do you hold the irrational belief that you and/ or your environment must be perfect, at all times?

Do you strive to be the best, to reach the ideal or goal and to never make a mistake?

Do you believe that it is what you achieve not who you are that is important?

Are you preoccupied with the fear of failure or with fears about not being able to sustain success?

Do you become overly defensive or emotional when criticized?

According to the dictionary, perfectionism is a belief that perfection can and should be attained. Perfectionists believe that mistakes can **never** be made and that the highest standards of performance must always be achieved.

Unproductive Behaviors of Perfectionism

Perfectionism causes unproductive behaviors such as procrastination, competition, judgment of themselves and others, all or nothing thinking and obsessive-compulsiveness. In order to maintain the perfect personae, they typically have to make others lose or look bad in some way. Accordingly, many people with perfectionist mindsets have a difficult time sustaining relationships.

Make a list of your behaviors that are consistent with a perfectionist mindset.

_____

_____

_____

Most perfectionists believe that they need to be perfect to be worthy of love and acceptance. Hard as they may try though, in the end, no one is perfect and the sad reality is even when you are the "best," it doesn't guarantee acceptance and love.

Someone that believes they must be perfect in order to be loved and accepted actually isolates themselves from the love and acceptance they desire.

Everything is viewed as a competition, where the perfectionist must emerge victorious. If not, they believe they will be rejected. So perfectionists may procrastinate, making excuses like "I don't have all the research completed yet" or "I don't have time to work on this project because I'm busy with other more pressing tasks." Another perfectionist belief that could cause procrastination or other irrational behavior is "If I achieve my goal, maybe I won't be able to maintain that same level of success."

Take Jim, an excellent sales person, for example. He ran away from three high paying jobs in a five year period. Every time he became the top salesperson, he would leave his job and move on to another company. Why? He was a perfectionist and lived in fear of being knocked out of the number one position on the sales team, which he perceived as humiliating.

Once we started working together, he realized fear of rejection, from an "I am not good enough" core belief, resulted in his perfectionist mindset. This thinking was driving him to make the career changes. He thought he might not be accepted and admired if someone else sold more than him. So his solution? Quit, run away, escape before that could happen!

Through coaching, he was able to recognize this destructive pattern for what it was and now he's been at the same company for three years! He's been in and out of the top salesperson spot several times and each time it gets easier for him. He recognizes now that his accomplishments do not determine his worth.

He's begun to love himself unconditionally. He's realized that coming from a place of love has resulted in deeper relationships with his co-workers and the acceptance that he never really received when his only goal was to be number one.

Most perfectionists are also their own worst critics. They constantly berate themselves if they haven't lived up to their hopelessly high standards. This judgmental behavior then carries over to their assessment of others. As much as the perfectionist yearns for love and acceptance, their judgmental nature pushes people away. It's also difficult for someone else to live up to the high standards of the perfectionist. In addition, the perfectionist needs to be the best, so many times they judge others harshly as a way of making themselves feel better.

Have you noticed that when you criticize others, it is in fact, a reflection of behaviors that you don't like within yourself? Think about the last time you had a judgmental thought about someone else; what was the message for you? What do you think about it NOW?

_____

_____

_____

_____

_____

_____

Release Perfectionism

Perfectionism is a mindset typically developed in childhood, especially in homes that practice an authoritarian parenting style combined with conditional love. The child, by being constantly vigilant and trying extremely hard, could exercise some aspect of control to ensure that they were not disappointments to their parents, thus avoiding whatever repercussions their parent favored, maybe yelling, name calling, or some other type of emotional or physical abuse. Many also worked to become beyond reproach and protect themselves against unforeseen issues which laid the groundwork for their perfectionist mindset. Maintaining those behaviors is a lot of pressure for a child, all in the name of receiving love and acceptance. In the end, these children grew up with firmly established limiting core beliefs, such as: "I am not enough", "I am not capable" or "I am not lovable."

Now, as adults, it doesn't really matter how we came to hold a perfectionist mindset, what does matter is letting go of the destructive behaviors. To release perfectionism, we must give ourselves permission to be human; allow ourselves to be perfectly imperfect, to make mistakes, and yes, even allow someone else to be right occasionally!

It's about love and realizing that nothing, absolutely nothing, has to be done to be worthy of love. You are worthy, it's your right as a human being and child of God. Forgive your parents or other care givers, knowing that they did the best they could do at the time and truly did love you. Make the choice to love yourself today.

You can ease up, starting NOW, by realizing that no one is perfect; no kidding, really, no one! You can make a mistake and it's OK. Your house can be a mess when someone drops by unexpectedly and it's OK. You don't have to be the best golfer to have fun in a golf league.

You can also give up all or nothing thinking and allow for some middle ground. You are not either perfect or worthless. You are not either number one or a failure. You don't allow one cookie to lead to a dozen because you were "bad." That type of thinking is over!

Use the Transformations Breakthrough Process™ found in Appendix A, to begin to release perfectionism from your life. You cannot ignite your inner power when you are living with a perfectionist mindset so be sure to take the time to do this exercise.

One typical perfectionist thought pattern is beating yourself up over mistakes. You can use the strategy found at the end of this chapter when you have made a mistake and cannot shake it. The more you become aware of your perfectionist actions when they are occurring, the quicker you will be able to shift your behaviors to those that are more productive for your life.

Summary: The Perfectionist

Core Beliefs: "I'm not lovable", "I'm not capable", "I'm not enough"

Mindset: I must act and be perfect at all times to show that I am lovable, capable or enough.

Thoughts:

"Don't make a mistake, that would be unacceptable."

"Better double check your work."

"Get the house cleaned and don't forget to do the top of the refrigerator, so and so is coming over."

Emotion: FEAR

Actions: Procrastination, making everything into a competition, lack of motivation, over focused on rules and details, paralysis regarding projects, compulsiveness

Vibration: Insecurity, unworthiness, anger, disgust, doubt, worry, frustration, pessimism, guilt

Strategy

When you realize you are in a situation where you feel the urge to be the best or do everything you possibly can to avoid making a mistake, or maybe you've already made a mistake, follow this process.

First, identify the feeling that is present right now, when you think of this circumstance. Use the emotional scale found on page 101 to work your way back into a positive emotion, using the technique you will learn in Chapter 9. When doing the following exercise, it's best to be in a high vibration energy.

Now that you are feeling empowered, say out loud or strongly in your mind's voice:

I release the critical thought that I am _____ (bad, unworthy, undeserving, unlovable, etc.) because I _____ (insert the specific belief, thought or action).

For example, I release the critical thought that I am inadequate because I didn't hit the golf ball well off the tee during this round. (Golf is a great analogy to life in general; I live on a golf course and am married to a golf instructor so I've watched many people throw golf clubs over a stupid game! But honestly, what I've found, is how they act on the golf course is how they act in their life.)

Then replace your disempowering thought with an affirmation, such as I am enough just as I am (and choose to have FUN in my life, especially on the golf course).

Your new affirmation is:

_____

_____

Remember, releasing judgments does not mean denying responsibility for your actions. It just means not labeling yourself in a derogatory way and then carrying that label around into everything else that you do.

You can also symbolically release this event using one of the techniques in Appendix B.

Chapter 5
The Instant Gratification Mindset

Instant gratification is a mindset that holds many people back from achieving their dreams. They may know what they want but can't seem to find it within themselves to do what it takes to achieve it. Do you identify with any of these?

Do you have money saved up for retirement or in a rainy day fund?

Do you set a goal to change a certain behavior and then each day you begin, but something happens to throw you off course?

If you want to make a purchase, such as a new widescreen plasma TV, do you save the money and purchase it with cash or do you buy it now with a credit card?

Do you eat fast food rather than taking the time to cook healthy meals?

Do you watch TV in the evenings instead of playing with your children, spending time with your significant other, exercising, meditating, or nurturing yourself in some way?

According to the dictionary, gratification is experiencing a source of satisfaction or pleasure. Instant gratification is receiving that pleasure immediately whereas delayed gratification is waiting in order to obtain what you want. People with an instant gratification mindset believe that their needs must to be satisfied NOW; they subconsciously perceive pain is involved in waiting and so they opt for the immediate pleasure. But wait, I know what you are thinking; wouldn't we all rather experience pleasure? Sure, we would, but those with a delayed gratification mindset consciously decide to wait for their pleasure and don't perceive the waiting time as painful.

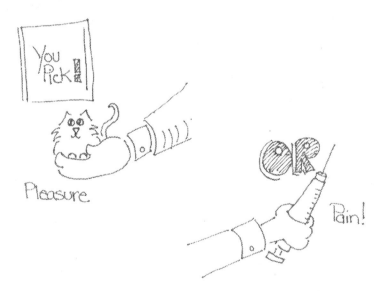

Unproductive Behaviors of Instant Gratification

Some of the unproductive behaviors caused by the instant gratification mindset include over spending, short-term thinking, preference for the quick fix, tendency to give up if results are not seen quickly, excessive pleasure seeking, and impatience. People who hold the immediate gratification mindset frequently experience failure or lack of success in the long-term. This is because the immediate satisfaction of a need typically causes detrimental long-term consequences. For example, an overweight person who chooses to watch TV every evening instead of exercising will ultimately face health challenges from this choice.

Make a list of your behaviors that are consistent with an instant gratification mindset.

_____

_____

_____

Did you include jockeying between check-out lines at the grocery store, darting in and out of traffic, eating whenever you have the urge, and even opening presents before Christmas morning? Texting, instant messaging, or writing on someone's Facebook wall to stay in constant communication are some of the ways technological advances over the last decades are encouraging us to exhibit instant gratification. With the dramatic changes we've experienced, we're losing our ability to wait. We expect instant results and many of us become impatient when we are required to wait, even a few minutes. Astute businesses are noticing and doing their best to please us, only compounding the problem. For example, Starbucks recently added instant coffee to their menu to accommodate customers who apparently don't have three to five minutes to wait for the real thing! If you can relate to the instant gratification behaviors I've mentioned, don't take it personally, we are becoming an instant gratification society.

The core limiting belief held by many people with the instant gratification mindset is "I don't deserve." They hold this subconscious belief that they don't deserve and so the instant gratification mindset is created to protect them from feeling unworthy. Just as the perfectionist mindset is created to prove someone lovable or capable, the instant gratification mindset is created to prove someone worthy or deserving.

I deserve to relax and enjoy myself watching TV *{rather than read a book about investing}*; I deserve to have this expensive new watch right now *{rather than wait for 6 months while I save the money}*; I deserve to have this daily café mocha for $3.49/day *{rather than purchase a gym membership for $39/ mo}*. These are the thoughts generated by the instant gratification mindset; the portion of each statement in brackets may not be considered by the individual. Their conscious thought is basically, "go ahead, you deserve it."

Michelle loved to spend money on new clothes and frequently needed an entirely new wardrobe each season because her clothes from last season didn't fit. She always paid for the new items with her charge cards. Shopping was fun for her; she felt great when she went into a store and tried on the latest styles and typically frequented her favorite store every ten days. During coaching, she told me that she always had a story about why she needed to buy something: "I need this outfit to look good at an upcoming meeting", "I have to have something new to wear to the wedding next month!" or "My shorts from last summer are all too tight; I need four new pairs."

Michelle's income was not enough to support her spending habit and so her credit card balances grew every year. It took ten years for Michelle to accumulate credit card debt of about $35,000 with her instant gratification mindset and desire to build her self-confidence with sharp new clothes. She knew she needed to change her mindset now or she would not be able to recover from her habitual spending habits.

When Michelle realized that she could not continue on this way, she embarked on understanding the reasons behind her spending habits. She discovered her limiting core beliefs of being not deserving and not lovable. Those beliefs caused the creation of the instant gratification mindset that became her mode of operation. With this awareness, Michelle was able to create a new mindset of delaying gratification.

Her new mindfulness regarding delaying gratification has served her in other areas of her life as well. This past spring, when Michelle tried on her summer shorts from last year, she found they fit! No need for a new wardrobe this summer; her new mindset affected her eating choices, too.

Release Instant Gratification

The easiest way to release instant gratification is by becoming conscious! You can think more long term by paying attention to decisions as they are made, effectively staying in the moment throughtout your day. It's our subconscious nature to prefer pleasure over pain, so being mindful gives you the opportunity to really evaluate what's most important; a moment of short-term pleasure or the long-term benefit that is the result of waiting.

Think about how you drive your car today. If you're like me, you are totally unconscious. Have you ever had the experience of suddenly noticing where you are and thinking "Did I go through Maple Rapids already?" So many of us let that same behavior run our life. All day long we are bombarded with choices that can have long term consequences on our relationships, finances and health and we just zoom along on auto-pilot, letting our pleasure seeking subconscious take charge.

An alternative to this instant gratification mindset is to simply WAKE UP! When you consciously contemplate decisions, you are more likely to think about the benefits of choosing the path that takes patience before results materialize.

I suggest to my clients to stay in the moment by using the following saying at the point of decision:

I'm in control of my choices. Is this what I choose?

There's always a moment of choice before you make a decision. I've heard comments from clients such as: "I just go unconscious and before I know it I've eaten a quart of ice cream!" However, there is the second, before you "go unconscious", that you have the opportunity to make a different choice. Use that moment to remember you're in control of your choices. Once you remember you have the ability to choose, then consider the long-term result or goal desired and make your decision in the present moment.

In Chapter 9, you'll learn about Step 2 - Align, of the Conscious Transformation Process™. You'll discover how to use visualization and affirmations to keep your goals and desires present in your awareness. These techniques will help you remember what you truly desire so the decisions you make will support your intentions.

Developing a mindset that emphasizes the long-term effect of decisions is extremely important for your ultimate success. Rather than trying to fulfill needs immediately, looking for the latest fad diet or even falling for some get rich quick scheme, people who delay gratification recognize that achieving success or goals takes time and sometimes hard work. However, researchers have found that even though the short-term effect of exerting self-control depletes that limited energy resource, the more you practice self-control, the easier your ability to delay gratification becomes. It's like a muscle that develops with use.

Now instead of looking for quick and easy ways of making money, you invest in books, seminars, stocks or insurance products that will have future benefits. Over time you develop the patience to wait for greater abundance in the future. The delay gratification mindset will improve every aspect of your life; you'll have more thriving relationships, a healthier body, and greater career success, which will all lead to more abundance in your life.

You can use the Transformations Breakthrough Process™ found in Appendix A to release any limiting core beliefs you may have that are associated with instant gratification. The exercise that follows will also help you get started on adopting new delay gratification actions into your life.

Summary: Instant Gratification Mindset

Core Beliefs: "I don't deserve", "I'm not worthy"

Mindset: I can appear to be deserving and worthy by never denying myself.

Thoughts:

"I deserve to get this NOW."

"This is not working out; I'm out of here!"

"I want to lose ten pounds before next week; I'd better take that diet pill."

Emotion: FEAR

Actions: Over spending, short-term thinking, always looking for the quick fix, excessive pleasure seeking, impatient behaviors

Vibration: Insecurity, unworthiness, impatience, frustration, irritation, jealousy

Strategy

How many times have you made a commitment to yourself only to say "I can do that tomorrow?" Unfortunately, tomorrow becomes next week or maybe never comes at all.

It may seem like you are not hurting anyone by not keeping that commitment, but you are – you are hurting YOURSELF! Those broken commitments chip away at your self-esteem, self-respect and even at your sense of integrity. Does this seem odd since you were the only person involved? Maybe on a conscious level, but to your subconscious mind, these incongruencies are a very big deal. The subconscious mind becomes confused because it doesn't know what you really want.

For example, let's say you have chosen to BE healthy and commit to going to the gym on Monday, Wednesday and Friday at 6am. Then on Friday morning the little voice in your head says "Stay in bed; I'm tired. Just go tomorrow instead." So you stay home. Now your subconscious doesn't know if you want to BE healthy or if you want to spend more time sleeping. Knowing what you truly desire is a big part of activating the Law of Attraction and using the Conscious Transformation Process™.

So don't commit to things you won't do and when you do commit to something, actually do it.

To practice the delay gratification mindset, pick something that you aren't currently doing but know will move you forward towards achieving an important long term goal. Let's say you decide to forego your daily café mocha and instead save the $3.50/day. Make a commitment to doing that and then stick to it. Everyday put the $3.50 in a jar and deposit it at the end of the month. It's easy; just take the actions necessary every day to keep the commitment.

What do you want to commit to doing? What actions will you take?

_____

_____

_____

_____

_____

_____

NOW JUST DO IT!! YOU'LL FEEL GREAT ABOUT YOURSELF WHEN YOU DO.

Chapter 6
The Scarcity Mindset

The scarcity mindset is the final mindset we are going to examine. Individuals with this mindset have difficulty creating success in their lives because they inherently believe there is lack in their world. They always look outside of themselves for solutions to their "not enough" challenge. Do you identify with any of these?

Are you worried someone may take advantage of you?

Do you need to see HOW something is going to be accomplished before you will set a goal to achieve it?

Do you believe it takes money to make money?

Are you concerned with competitors stealing your customers or with someone taking your job?

Do you focus on what you don't have; money, customers, health, etc.?

People with scarcity mentality spend a great deal of time in "want to", "could" or "would do" thinking but not as much time in action. Their focus is typically on the problem they are experiencing and how it's affecting them rather than on creating a solution to the challenge. Their thoughts are about "not enough"; not enough customers, not enough sales, not enough money, not enough time, not enough good employees, not enough skills, not enough talent, not enough love and so on.

Unproductive Behaviors of the Scarcity Mentality

Some of the unproductive behaviors caused by scarcity mindset include blaming others for problems, complaining and whining while focusing on a problem or issue, not the solution, hoarding or protecting possessions, avoiding risks, and jealousy. A scarcity mentality implies that for someone to win, another person must lose; that resources are scarce and it's important to do what is necessary to get a share. In actuality, life is not a zero-sum game. There is plenty for everyone.

Years ago I worked as a district manager for a direct sales clothing company; my job was to recruit, train and motivate new fashion consultants. Within my territory there were a couple of large cities with populations, including suburbs, of over 300,000. An area like that could support four to five fashion consultants. I recruited a new consultant in one of the cities that already had two experienced fashion consultants in place. The existing consultants were upset, even though they knew I had been actively recruiting in their area. They were certain there wouldn't be enough customers to go around. In the end, I had to spend more time with the two original people coaching them out of their scarcity mindset than I spent training the new fashion consultant!

Individuals with scarcity mentality are quick to blame others for their issues. For example, one business person might blame a recession for a downturn in their business while another person in the same industry, obviously experiencing the same economic conditions, might dig in their heels, rework their product offerings and actually expand their business. It's interesting how the same set of circumstances affects people differently, isn't it?

Make a list of your behaviors that are consistent with a scarcity mindset.

_____

_____

_____

_____

Have you ever noticed that at the first prediction of a large snow storm people rush the grocery store? My workout buddy, Linda, says those people must know the recipe for a bread, milk and toilet paper casserole! In fact, anytime there's media attention on a shortage of anything, people with scarcity mentality make sure they get their fair share. During a beef shortage in the 1980s, spoiled, unopened packages of steaks were found at garbage dumps. Most likely purchased by scarcity minded individuals who typically tend to waste the very thing they are trying to hoard, such as, food, money, talent, love, etc.

The core limiting beliefs held by many people with a scarcity mindset are "I am not [good] enough" and "I don't deserve [because I am not enough]." Individuals with these core beliefs are worried that someone might take advantage of them; that their "not enough-ness" will be shown to the world. Deep down they believe that success might happen for other people but probably not for them. It's important for many people with these core beliefs to hold on tight to what they do have so that it doesn't get taken from them.

Individuals operating from a scarcity mindset blame other people and circumstances for challenges occurring in their life. Their thoughts include "I didn't cause this problem and so it's out of my hands to fix it." In this way, the person with scarcity mentality never has to demonstrate if they are good enough to deal with anything. They don't take responsibility for the issues in their life.

They are also unwilling to take action to improve their situation. They prefer to complain, refer to themselves as unlucky, and even ignore well thought out suggestions regarding changes they could make to their life. Unfortunately, they don't want to change or do something new because it's too big of a risk.

Jill and Jane are two friends that joined a network marketing company at the same time. When they first started, Jane made a comment to Jill about having a contest to see who could get to the level of

Take **100%** responsibility!!

consultant first. Jill's nature is non-competitive so she shrugged that comment off with the hope that they would both make consultant and continue to have fun.

Jill easily attracted some of her other friends to join her while Jane struggled to get her business off the ground. When they got together at meetings, Jane would make comments to Jill such as "You'll probably be a senior consultant before I make consultant." These comments always made Jill uncomfortable and she tried to explain to Jane that they weren't in a competition; she even offered to help her. Jane didn't attend the award ceremony when Jill received recognition for her advancement to Consultant and shortly thereafter, left the business.

Jane has a scarcity mindset; Stephen Covey, highly regarded author of *The 7 Habits of Highly Successful People*, noted that people with scarcity mentality have difficulty being genuinely happy for the success of other people, especially someone they know. Jane couldn't celebrate the success of her friend because somehow that success diminished her. Unfortunately, Jill and Jane's relationship has been permanently affected by this situation.

A person with the limiting belief that they are "not enough" may be living in a world of lack, but their scarcity mindset focuses on blaming someone else for what they don't have. They play the part of victim and claim they can't do anything about it. Of course, in their mind, they're not the cause of the lack they are experiencing. Just as the fashion consultants in my earlier example wanted to blame the company for the downturn they were predicting would occur when the new consultant was added to their city.

Release Scarcity Mentality

In what areas of your life do you hold the scarcity mindset?

_____

_____

_____

_____

_____

_____

_____

_____

_____

_____

_____

_____

_____

_____

An important first step in replacing a scarcity mindset with an abundance mindset is to become aware of and focus on all of the abundance already occurring in our lives. Just look around at all the abundance in the Universe that's available to you. Go to the grocery store and look at the produce aisle. Walk in a garden and see the abundance of flowers and insects. Notice all the people in your life: friends, family and acquaintances.

What you focus on expands. If you are short on money right now, instead of thinking about that, focus on the abundance of possibilities that are available to make money. Before you know it, ideas and opportunities will start to show up in your consciousness.

Another excellent strategy for replacing scarcity is to practice gratitude for what you do have. You can notice and appreciate the place where you live, the resources that are available to you, the sun, water and air, the food that you take for granted, and the friends and family that are your support system, just to name a few.

As you practice appreciation, also be selective with what you put into your mind. Don't allow media and advertising to affect your decisions. Instead, read, listen to and watch personal development material. Spend time with people like Jill; people with an abundance mindset. To create your own internal environment of abundance, choose what you are exposed to wisely. If you are experiencing a contraction regarding money right now, remember when you had abundance. By reminding yourself of those times, you will realize that you can create that again in your life.

In the next section of this book, you'll learn to use the Conscious Transformation Process™ to attract the outcomes you desire. You can also use that technique to BE abundant and leave the scarcity mindset behind.

Summary: Scarcity Mentality

Core Beliefs: "I am not enough", "I don't deserve", "I'm not worthy"

Mindset: If I avoid responsibility for everything in my life and hold on tight to everything I have, I'll appear good enough.

Thoughts:

"That might work for some people, but not for me."

"I think someone is taking advantage of me!"

"That new competitor that opened down the street is driving me out of business."

Emotion: FEAR

Actions: Blaming others, complaining and whining instead of getting into action, hoarding and protecting possessions, risk avoidance, jealousy

Vibration: Stress, struggle, despair, unworthiness, anxiety, frustration, irritation, jealousy

Strategy

At the end of each day, write down three examples of abundance that you noticed and appreciated during that day.

1. _____
   _____
   _____

2. _____
   _____
   _____

3. _____
   _____
   _____

If you are experiencing any scarcity mindset feelings, use your breath to release them. You can breathe out the old limiting scarcity mindset that you want to release and breathe in the abundance mindset. For example: Breathe out lack, breathe in abundance; breathe out struggle, breathe in ease; breathe out "I'm not enough", breathe in, "I am enough."

Establish this as a tradition every day and the abundance in your life will EXPAND TREMENDOUSLY!!

Conscious
Transformation
Process

Chapter 7
Manifesting Your Desires

It seems that at some point in our lives we all have thoughts that life will be so much better when we acquire a certain possession, have more money or become involved in a particular type of relationship, don't we? "If only I had _____, then I'd do _____, and I'll BE _____." You fill in the blanks. Some examples include:

"If only I had a husband, then I could go to the places where my couple friends go and I'll be fulfilled."

"When I have money, I'll do good works and be a philanthropist."

"If I had success, I could travel regularly and I'd be happy."

"If I had fewer pounds on my body, I could attract someone wonderful into my life and I'd be thrilled."

"When I am working in my dream job, I'll have more time to do things with my kids and then I'll be an attentive parent."

Can you identify with any of these? They are examples of the Have-Do-Be model. Unfortunately, many people are caught up in the "if only" mentality that implies that once we have something our life will magically change and then we'll be what we want.

Have you figured out yet that life doesn't work that way? Sad, but true.

I remember when I first understood this reality. My husband and I bought a sports car in the 1970s, a Datsun 260Z. What a sharp car, a powder blue beauty. It was my dream car!

Guess what I found out? Sitting in the car felt like being in any other car, except possibly a bit less comfortable. Were other people impressed by the fact we had such a fabulous car? Not really. In fact, I noticed that my life didn't change at all; I didn't become a happy, self-confident person suddenly because I acquired my dream car. Lucky for me, I was in my mid-20s when I discovered, through this experience, that if you don't first feel it on the inside, nothing is going to change when you acquire a new house, car or boat, wife or husband, dream job or business, or even lose 50 pounds.

The good news is you can have what you seek easily by reversing the Have-Do-Be model. It becomes Be-Do-Have and actually, that's how life really works!

Write about when you first discovered that material possessions did not give you fulfillment.

_____

_____

The Be-Do-Have Model

First you decide what or how you want to BE. How cool is that? You get to pick what you want to BE – maybe it's prosperous, healthy, joyful, mindful or happy. Basically, you get to choose to BE successful - whatever that means to you!

You see, being is just a decision. You decide and then commit to it. Have you ever been around someone who's unhappy as a result of an experience in their life, say a divorce? Suddenly, they wake up one day and decide the wallowing is over and they choose to BE happy. Nothing outside of them changed; they changed how they wanted to BE on the inside.

Take Marcia, for example, an artist for most of her life. However, for the 14 years following her divorce, Marcia stopped painting. Unable to pinpoint the exact reasons why, she felt blocked whenever she tried to channel her creative urges onto the canvas. As the years passed, she began to get rid of her supplies. When friends asked if she'd started painting again, she'd say, "Ever since my marriage ended, I can't paint."

Several months ago, Marcia watched the movie "The Secret" and felt moved by its message. As she considered her "I can't paint" thought, she realized that she had made this limiting belief her reality. Like a light bulb suddenly flashing above her head, she understood she had the power to release the belief and replace it with a mindset that better suited the life she wanted to experience. Pushing all traces of "I can't paint" from her head, Marcia thought triumphantly, "I choose to BE a painter!"

That day was a turning point for Marcia. Since then, she's transformed the sunroom of her home into a welcoming, light-filled studio, found a friend to paint there with her, and is busily engaged in plans to create a painting for each of her ten grandchildren. Marcia said she's noticed a difference in other areas of her life as well. She feels more energized, freer. Says Marcia, "This is a happy story. For the first time in years, I finally feel settled."

You see BEING is actually energetic reality. It comes from your mind only. We'll talk more about BEING in the Conscious Transformation Process™ Steps 1 and 2, Announce and Align.

The actions you take come from the BEING you decide upon. I tell my weight release clients "You can't choose to BE healthy and then eat (DO) a dozen cookies every day." That's incongruent behavior. Your actions must be congruent with your BEING. We'll discuss DOING in the Conscious Transformation Process™ Steps 3 and 4, Act and Account.

Finally, once you choose to BE something and DO congruent behaviors, guess what happens? Right!! You get to HAVE what you want in physical reality. And it's so much more than a car, house or spouse. It's more than you can ever imagine because you've ignited your inner power. We'll take a look at HAVING in the Conscious Transformation Process™ Step 5, Allow.

In the next chapters, you will learn how to apply the BE-Do-Have model in your life using the Conscious Transformation Process™. Are you ready to make this shift in your thinking; a shift that can change everything? It changed my life and I'm confident it will change yours as well.

Chapter 8
Step 1: Announce
Announce What You Want

What Do You Want to BE?

The first step in this process is very clearly deciding and defining exactly what you want. What do you want? I've found there is a big difference between people who want to lose weight, obtain more money, or find a spouse and those who want to BE Healthy, BE Prosperous or BE Intimately Connected! The people in the first category only want to get something and fail for a couple of predictable reasons. First, they are short-term thinkers, usually looking for a quick fix, which never works.

Second, they start with actions first. Think for a minute about life-long dieters. They go from one quick fix diet to another, whatever the latest fad, but in the end, they never find anything that really works. In fact, with each new diet, the end result is that most gain back more weight than they lost. It's because they are starting with the "doing" first, instead of the "being."

The bottom line is that individuals who choose what they want to "BE" first, make changes that enable long-term success and permanent change. Being

healthy, happy or prosperous is an internal state; it's energetic reality as I mentioned in an earlier chapter. It has nothing to do with your current situation and nothing outside of you needs to happen or exist in order to make this decision.

In my workshops, I survey people, asking them if they were informed that they were receiving a $10,000 inheritance from a long lost relative, would they feel abundant, 1) when they found out they had the money coming, 2) when they received the check or 3) when they deposited the check. When would you feel abundant? If you are like 95% of the population, you chose option 1, when you initially FOUND out about the inheritance. Being abundant has nothing to do with actually having money in a bank account. The same is true of being healthy or happy. It's a feeling you create.

Once you say "Yes" to the BEING you've selected, don't sabotage your decision with contradictory thoughts, just BE. Your thoughts should be those of a person who already IS what you want to BE. Feel as if you are healthy, happy, prosperous, etc., regardless of what your current physical situation is right now.

I'm reminded of Einstein's famous quote:

> *"The definition of insanity is doing the same thing over and over again and expecting a different result."*

You can't choose to BE healthy, wealthy or happy, but continue to DO the same things you've always done. However, in this step of the process, just focus on the BEING. The DOING will come later.

Sue, a young physician with two children, felt burdened by her seemingly insurmountable medical school debt. She loved the practice she worked at and her patients but wondered if she should leave for a higher paying position. Unsure how she'd find the money she needed to pay off her debt, Sue decided to trust the Conscious Transformation Process™ and stated her intention to satisfy her debt with ease; she declared herself to BE debt free.

Within weeks, Sue received a job offer from a hospital nearby, with debt repayment built into the compensation package. It was a mixed blessing because Sue wasn't excited about the hospital facility but the debt repayment benefit was impossible to pass up. After approaching her existing employer with the news that she would have to leave the practice, she was thrilled to get and accept a counteroffer including both loan payoff and a healthy raise. Today, Sue continues to find joy at work in the practice she loves and is free of her money worries, all because she chose to BE debt free.

What do you want to BE?

_____

_____

_____

Why Do You Want to BE What You've Chosen?

Now it's time to analyze why you want to BE in the new state of BEING you've chosen. In the spaces below write down all of the reasons you have made this decision. Keep writing until you have all of your reasons listed.

1) _____   10) _____

2) _____   11) _____

3) _____   12) _____

4) _____   13) _____

5) _____   14) _____

6) _____   15) _____

7) _____   16) _____

8) _____   17) _____

9) _____   18) _____

The next step is to see if you are motivated by fear or love. For example, is it love of health and all that brings to your life or the fear of being unattractive? If it's fear, you may not feel good about yourself at the present moment; you might compare your body to someone else's and feel inferior. You may be worried about what other people think of you.

What sort of feelings do fear-based thoughts generate? Low energy, right! They keep you from having total faith in your ability to manifest your desires and typically block you from receiving your intention to become healthy, using this example. Fear based thoughts will continue to create more unwanted feelings which will ultimately hamper your motivation to put into practice new behaviors.

If, instead, your intention is coming from love and is connected to your values, you are guaranteed to receive your desire with the least effort applied. You will be able to harness the power of love and easily manifest your desire. Remember, like attracts like. When you generate joyful, loved based feelings about your healthy body, abundance, happiness, etc., you will attract even more high energy feelings.

Love based reasons are considered inner motivators because achieving your desire will impact you personally and your quality of life. Fear based reasons are outer motivators; achieving your desire will supposedly affect how someone else views or treats you.

So take a moment now, to review your reasons and identify which are from love and which are from fear. Count the number of reasons you have that are love based and the number that are fear based. Which do you have more of, love or fear?

Many spiritual teachers agree that when we achieve something that we sought due to fear, it doesn't last. Why? It doesn't last because we are afraid of losing what we obtained. Our disempowering thoughts sabotage us! Studies show that women who were successful dieting, but were motivated by fear continue to compare themselves to others and live in fear of regaining the weight they lost. The same goes for people who have acquired the money they desired. If they were not motivated by love, they live in a constant state of fear that they will lose their wealth. When your focus is external and fear based, you'll always be disappointed.

Psychologist and author Joan Borysenko states in *The Power of the Mind to Heal* that the purpose of life is learning to transform fear into love. So don't be too hard on yourself if you have fear-based reasons; we all have them and now that you've brought them to your awareness, transforming them can lead to wonderful personal growth possibilities! See Appendix A for the Transformations Breakthrough Process™ that you can use to work through your limiting beliefs.

Clarify Your Intention

Now that you have determined your reasons for wanting to BE healthy, prosperous, or happy, with ideal relationships and successful careers or businesses, let's turn our attention to all the components of that BEING you'd like to attract into your life.

To help my clients clarify their intentions, I designed the Contrast Brings Clearness™ form, which you'll find at the end of this chapter. The objective is to arrive at a list of "What I Do Want:" on the top portion of this form. However, you might find it is easier to clarify what you do want if you briefly observe what you don't want, or the contrast, then you can reframe those into what you do want.

To get clear about what you do want, start by writing down everything you don't want to experience

Get Clear

Let the Universe know what you Desire!

related to your new state of BEING in the "I don't want" bottom section; many of these unhappy realities are in your life now. Then you reframe those "I don't wants" into what you do want by asking yourself "What is it that I do want?" and write that in the "What I Do Want" top section of the worksheet.

To help you understand how to complete this form, let's use Cheryl as an example; she's a woman from a workshop that wanted to attract a new job. The first step is to complete the "What Is It You Want?; My Ideal _____", in the header of the Contrast Brings Clearness form. The state of BEING that Cheryl wanted to get clear about was to BE a fulfilled employee and so she wrote "My Ideal Fulfilling Job".

Next, complete the bottom shaded section that is labeled "What I Don't Want." Think about what you don't want. For example, here are some things Cheryl wrote that she did not want:

Overnight travel

Unhappy co-workers

A long commute

Boring, tedious work.

Of course, your list will be much longer and as you work in this process, you may think of more and more, so just keep adding to the list as something comes to mind. To do the reframe, take each item, one at a time and restate what you do want as a positive statement, and write it in the top section of the form. "Overnight travel" is Cheryl's first. Watch your words to make sure you don't inadvertently say something negative. For example, "No overnight travel" would not be an appropriate reframe because your unconscious mind does not recognize not and no's. So the only thing understood is travel overnight, which is exactly what Cheryl didn't want. An appropriate reframe is "To be home every evening." The reframe for "Unhappy co-workers" could be "Happy co-workers." The reframe for "A long commute" could be "To work a short distance from home" and for "Boring, tedious work" the reframe Cheryl chose was "Interesting, challenging work."

Now it's your turn to thoughtfully complete the Contrast Brings Clearness™ worksheet. To obtain the contrast items, think about what you don't like experiencing related to your state of BEING right now. Then reframe those items in the "What I Do Want..." section. After you have those identified, continue writing more "What I Do Want..." as you start to flow with ideas of what you want. Ask yourself what traits and aspects of this state of BEING you want to attract to your life. Complete the Contrast Brings Clearness™ worksheet found on the last page of this chapter or download a copy from my website and work with that: www.choosesuccessbook.com/Resources.html.

Once you have completed the Contrast Brings Clearness™ exercise, fold the paper on the dotted line, so you only have the "What I Do Want..." section in view. This represents the essence of what you want and what you focus on.   Feel free to add more items to your list.

Cheryl got a job offer within one week of completing her form and when she reviewed the Contrast Brings Clearness™ form, she realized this job offered her everything she asked for. However, she didn't want the job! She discovered, from this opportunity, some new items to add to her top section of what she did want; for example, weekends free.

Summary

Physician Deepak Chopra, in his book, *The Seven Spiritual Laws of Success,* says the future is created in the present by your intentions. According to Chopra, you must accept the present and intend the future. You can do it! In addition, author Gregg Braden, in *The Divine Matrix,* states "We have all the power we need to create all the changes we choose." Now that you've chosen your state of BEING and clarified your desires and intentions, you'll see the changes begin.

Contrast Brings Clearness
What is it you want?

My Ideal _____

What I Do Want:

_____

_____

_____

_____

_____

_____

_____

_____

_____

_____

What I Don't Want:

Chapter 9
Step 2: Align
Align with What You Want

Once you know what you want, the next step is to align yourself and your vibration with that. Really see yourself having what you want, in all areas of your life.

I teach clients to look at alignment in two ways. First, keeping your overall energy high is important in this process. You can't be constantly fighting with your spouse and expect to manifest a healthy life or abundance. Second, keeping your energy high related to the particular thing you want to manifest helps you maintain belief and faith in the process.

The Energy Barometer, located at the end of this chapter and also on my website at www. choosesuccessbook.com/Resources.html, monitors overall energy. It's similar to the Wheel of Life, if you are familiar with that tool, but from a vibrational point of view since it is designed to use feelings to measure your energy in each category.

Usually, maintaining balance and high energy in all aspects of your life is preferable. However, this does not mean you should ignore or devalue your feelings. Understanding your emotions is crucial to discovering your core beliefs and mindsets that might be limiting you.

Refer to page 101 now, or print The Energy Barometer found on my website, and use this tool to determine your present energy levels. There are three color coded spokes for each aspect of your life: blue is for Body, green is for Mental/Emotional and the red is for Spirit.

Go through each spoke and rate your current energy level in that specific area based on the Emotion Perception Scale provided. Notice how the scale has love at the top and fear at the bottom, with examples of possible feelings positioned between those two true emotions. The feelings on the scale are just possibilities for you to consider; you may describe your actual feeling differently, so just select the feeling that most closely represents yours.

For example, there is a spoke called Exercise. Ask yourself "How do I feel when I think about exercise in my life?" It could be frustration (an 8 on the scale) because you can't seem to stick to an exercise routine. Or you might be feeling optimism (a 3 on the scale) because you just found a new Zumba class in your area and absolutely love it, so you know you'll continue with that.

The goal is to have your overall vibration average 5 or less. That is why the row 5 with Hopefulness and Anticipation is highlighted on the Emotion Perception Scale. That's the entry level to higher vibration feelings. You can do several things with this tool; first, you can add all 9 categories together and divide by 9 to get your overall average. An average of 5 or lower is ideal for manifesting.

Another way of looking at it is to add all the Body spokes together and divide by 3, then do the same for the Mind/Emotion and Spirit spokes. This helps you see if you are out of balance in any one particular area. You'll find more information about how body, mind, and spirit are inter-related in the Energy Management section of this book.

The barometer helps you monitor your emotional vibration at any one point in time. Use it regularly. If you find any area, let's say "Exercise" where you have a lower vibration, then you can work specifically in that category to bring your vibration up. I teach people to work their way up the Emotion Perception Scale by reaching for higher thoughts.

Here's an Example of How this Might Work.

Let's say right now you are at "11 – Blame and Disgust" regarding exercise. Try to get into this feeling - you're disgusted with yourself because you know that exercise works but for some reason you just can't seem to get yourself motivated to do any exercise. Is there a thought that could bring you up to the level of disappointment?

How about *"I'm disappointed that I can't follow through on my good intentions to start exercising."* OK, how does that feel? Say it out loud and really feel the energy behind it.

Next, perhaps you could move to pessimism with the following thought: *"I'd like to join a gym but I know from past experience that I probably wouldn't stick with it."* Then, from pessimism let's move up the scale to hopefulness. *"Maybe I could find a partner to be my workout buddy and we could schedule*

regular workout times." Do you see how your energy and vibration shifted as we moved up the Emotion Perception Scale?

Use this technique of moving up the scale anytime you feel yourself generating low vibration energy about something. However, be sure to make gradual movements in thought. You can't go from feeling disgusted with yourself to suddenly saying *"Oh, I just love myself so much."* You'll never believe that statement because it's too big of a jump. This technique uses the theory of cognitive behavior therapy; reaching for a better feeling by creating believable thoughts that generate that emotion. So as you move up the scale, make sure you believe the thoughts you create.

Once you have an overall high vibration, next it's important to get excited and have positive energy surrounding the accomplishment of the specific thing you are trying to manifest; the state of BEING you have chosen.

"It's cancer, and we think it's aggressive. It may already be in your lymph nodes," Linda's doctors told her after finding abnormalities in her mammogram. Linda turned inward to ponder her next steps, while waiting several weeks for the lumpectomy.

She visualized herself as strong and healthy and worked to raise her vibration, never letting go of her belief the cancer could be contained and eliminated from her life. Linda viewed this "dis"-ease as her body's way of clearing out old issues and honored its message to love and trust herself more fully.

After the lumpectomy, Linda's doctors told her the surgery was a success. Additionally, to their surprise, the cancer had not spread to her lymph nodes after all.

Today, Linda remains cancer-free. Reflecting back on her experience, she says, "It's okay to experience negative thoughts and emotions when dealing with life's challenges. However, the key is recognizing that you can move yourself up the Emotion Perception Scale – one step at a time, and you'll get there. In the end, high vibration emotions are so much healthier for you and can create a wonderful result, like mine!"

Linda is so right. It is important to recognize and honor your low vibration feelings. Have you heard the saying "It's all good"? Judging our vibrations as positive or negative is the same as thinking of them as bad or good. Anytime we are judging or labeling something about ourselves or our habits, it's a slippery slope to taking on the label. My feeling is bad, so I am bad. My eating was bad, so I am bad for eating that. I overspend which is bad, so I am bad. Do you see what I mean?

Your feelings truly are "all good." As I mentioned earlier, lower energy feelings can help you discover limiting beliefs and learn important lessons. Stuffing your emotions down or purposely not feeling the emotions you are experiencing NEVER leads to learning or growth as a person. However, staying in lower vibration for long lengths of time means you are giving your power away to someone or some situation. That's not in your best interest either. Use the technique you just learned once you have examined your feeling and discovered the lesson.

Let's now turn to some ways that you can align with the particular outcome you desire.

Affirmations

One of the most powerful ways to structure your thoughts, engage your subconscious, and transform your goals into results, is with the use of affirmations. Affirmations are a big part of aligning with your intention.

Affirmations are positive statements, repeated over and over. They are used to make changes in health, happiness, relationships, prosperity, etc. Affirmations are words that have tremendous power over our minds! We're constantly talking to ourselves, sometimes repeating old negative patterns from our past which can limit our current success. Affirmations can cancel or correct those negative thoughts or ideas and instead create a belief in our ability to attain our goals and become the person we want to be.

The following five items represent the correct elements or components of a good affirmation:

1. Present tense – your affirmation needs to be presented to your mind as if it has already been achieved. An ineffective affirmation is *"I am working on becoming healthy and vibrant"*, instead say *"I am healthy and vibrant."*

2. Positive statement – always state your affirmation in positive terms. Don't focus on what you don't want. Your subconscious doesn't really know all the words, just what you focus on, so you end up with more of what you don't want. For example, if I say, "don't think about cake," what's the first thing that pops into your mind? CAKE! So don't affirm *"I don't want to be unhappy."* Instead say, *"I am happy."*

3. Short and specific – make your affirmation easy to say. Short affirmations have a greater impact on your subconscious than long and wordy ones. The short affirmation is easy to remember and your mind takes it in easier. *"I make healthy food choices."* is short and specific instead of *"I now enjoy eating foods that are naturally sweetened, organically grown and good for me."*

4. About you – start your affirmation with the word "I." You can't write an affirmation for anyone else and the "I" makes it very powerful.

5. Emotionally charged – use mood words to suggest strong and highly charged emotions or repeat your affirmation with enthusiasm

and joy in your voice. The more emotionally charged you make your affirmation, the stronger your vibration becomes.

Affirmations, when worded correctly and emotionally charged, are able to tap into the unlimited creative potential of your subconscious mind and manifest your goals and desires.

Susan didn't know what to try next. It had been over a year and her daughter still refused to speak to her. Nothing she did seemed to make a difference. Then Susan read Dr. Wayne Dyer's wonderful book, *There's a Spiritual Solution to Every Problem* and something about its message resonated with her.

Following the book's lead, Susan began affirming that she had a loving, healthy relationship with her daughter. She held this upbeat affirmation in her mind and repeated it every day. Others told her it wouldn't work, that she was setting herself up for failure. But Susan held firm to her belief.

Within three months, Susan's daughter contacted her. Today, they have reunited and Susan knows first-hand how powerful affirmations can be.

Create an affirmation to use in your quest to BE your desired new state. Your affirmation is:

_____

_____

_____

_____

Once you've created a snappy affirmation, repeat it over and over so that it imprints into your subconscious mind. You should repeat your affirmation about 30 times daily. Some people like to write out their affirmation, 30 times on a piece of paper. Others carry note cards or put post-it notes with their affirmations all over their house and/or car and when they see it, they repeat it over and over. I like to say affirmations when exercising, walking in the woods or driving my car.

Optimally, each month, you could have two to three affirmations that support your intentions. Then the next month, continue with these or replace any or all that you believe you no longer need, with different affirmations.

Remember affirmations raise your energy when they carry emotion. So when repeating your affirmation, get involved, say it with enthusiasm and passion, like you really believe it will happen! Think about what the words mean and feel the excitement that you will feel when you achieve your goal. Without the passion and emotional connection, your affirmations become weak. You must feel within yourself that your goal has been achieved. One workshop participant once said "Affirmations are like telling the truth in advance." That's so true.

Sometimes, however, my clients feel a twinge inside when they say their affirmation. For example, if your affirmation is "I make $350,000 a year" and immediately after you repeat it, your brain says "Who are you kidding, you'll never earn that much money in one year", this is a good clue there is a disconnect between what you want and what you believe.

I use those hints to help my clients uncover the limiting beliefs that may be holding them back from achieving what they want in their lives. You can do this as well by documenting the thoughts and feelings that come up when you first start to say a certain affirmation. Look for patterns so you can see if there is a particular limiting belief, like "I don't deserve..." or "I'm not enough..." that needs to be released. Then use the Transformations Breakthrough Process™ in Appendix A to release those outdated beliefs.

Guided Imagery

The primary aim of guided imagery is to "gently guide" you to a state where your mind is calm, silent and still. Then, through visualization, either created internally or by following along on an imagery CD, the mind communicates with the body. Imagery is the biological connection between the mind and body. A visualization where you see yourself releasing weight or at your ideal weight, attracting your ideal mate or experiencing life with that person, or getting the job you want, programs the subconscious mind to do what you want later after the imagery session is over.

It has been proven over and over again that what you are imagining right now will be what your life gives you in the future. Very often our mental image is in conflict with what we want to accomplish. However, if you align your mental image with your intentions and affirmations, you create a powerful roadmap for your subconscious to deliver to you everything that you want and more!

"As a man thinketh, so he is."
Proverbs 23:7.

We become what we think or say. So do you think that someone who makes statements like "I can't seem to get a job I like" or "A moment on the lips, a lifetime on the hips!" can listen to a guided imagery CD and then attract the perfect job or release weight? NO, of course not! I see so many people sabotage their efforts inadvertently by repeating sayings like these without giving any thought to the affect they are having on their efforts!

In order to BE what you want, you must align all parts of yourself, including your words and vision of who you are. You must be able to see yourself as you want to be, believe in your ability to be successful, speak it, and hold the vision in your mind.

Every day spend some time visualizing yourself as you want to BE. Relax your mind and body with some deep breathing. As you continue breathing, you will become more receptive to the mental stimuli given and less critical of the information as it filters into your subconscious. Either listen to an imagery CD or create the images yourself, it doesn't matter. What does matter is that you actually feel the emotion as if you already had what you desire. Create a very vivid picture in your mind and put yourself in the picture.

I suggest that my clients, who have difficulty feeling their emotions during a visualization, first raise their vibration by working their way up the Emotion Perception Scale prior to the imagery session. So if you desire to BE an employee in a fulfilling job, like Cheryl from the last chapter, perhaps your feeling right now is #8-Frustration when you think about attracting this perfect job. Go from frustration to acceptance by thinking *"I accept that the job market is tight right now so it may take a few months to attract my perfect job."* Then go to #5-Hopefulness by thinking *"I am looking for a job in a field where there is high demand so I hope the perfect position comes to my attention soon."* Move up to #3-Optimism with a thought like *"I have many networking contacts in the industry and I'll bet when I contact them, someone will know of a job opening and refer me right away."* Once you are feeling this vibration, it's a perfect time to do your visualization exercise.

When your thoughts are focused on imagining success, your subconscious mind will direct your conscious mind and body toward that goal. Nothing else is possible!!

Another similar tool that you can use for aligning yourself with your goal is scripting. A script is just a few paragraphs (think of it as a story) that you write about the state of BEING you desire. What does it feel like? What does it look like? What are you experiencing? Where are you? What is unique about it? My clients view scripting as a written for of guided imagery because they are basically putting their visualization down on paper.

Vision Boards or Wish Books

Vision boards and wish books are really fun to create. You either take a poster board or some pages in a small journal and paste on it pictures you find that exemplify the life you desire. You may decide to include pictures of your perfect home, the material possessions you want to attract, people that represent relationships you'd like; have fun with it! You can even do these online now with actual photos.

I've used wish books for years; once when I moved, I found an old wish book from about 5 years earlier. Upon examination, I found I had attracted everything that I put in that book; a second home in a resort area, a wonderful man, and a business of my own.

Steve is a realtor who wanted to increase his sales and improve the quality of his life. When a friend introduced him to the principles of manifesting, Steve was intrigued and began applying its principles. In August 2007, Steve created a vision board containing pictures and descriptions of his goals. He included a photograph of an opulent home with the caption "My first large listing and successful sale of over $300,000." Steve also added his intention to "have three new clients per month that are motivated to buy or sell."

Steve started seeing results quickly, even in what was widely believed to be a down market. He attracted three new clients in November and another three in December. And that $300,000 sale he wanted? Steve got his first big listing in December - for $489,000 and sold it by the end of the next month.

Steve was successful so quickly because he had faith and belief in the process and himself. He didn't question it; he knew he would manifest his desires. When you have this much belief, once you've created your vision board or wish book, it's not necessary to look at your vision board daily. However, if you don't have complete belief in the process, then looking at your wish book or vision board daily will serve as a way of building your belief.

Summary

The tools discussed in this chapter give you some options for alignment. I encourage you to use affirmations daily and then supplement your efforts with either visualization, scripting, or visual aids, such as a wish book or vision board, whichever appeals to your style. If you enjoy writing, opt for creating scripts. If, on the other hand, you prefer listening, then an imagery CD, that you create or purchase, will definitely be for you. If you enjoy working with your hands, then a vision board or wish book will be fun for you to create and use. I also enjoy making affirmation movies using Windows Movie Maker. It's a perfect way to combine affirmations with a visual aspect and creating the movie itself is FUN!

Which tool you select is not as important as faithfully using the tool, reading it, listening to it or looking at it, EVERY DAY.

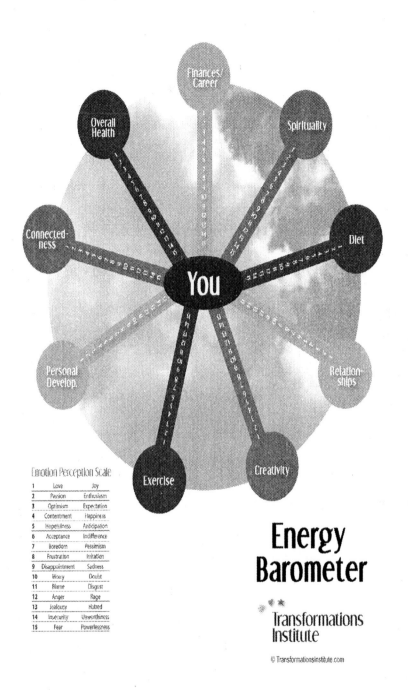

Emotion Perception Scale

1	Love	Joy
2	Passion	Enthusiasm
3	Optimism	Expectation
4	Contentment	Happiness
5	Hopefulness	Anticipation
6	Acceptance	Indifference
7	Boredom	Pessimism
8	Frustration	Irritation
9	Disappointment	Sadness
10	Worry	Doubt
11	Blame	Disgust
12	Anger	Rage
13	Jealousy	Hatred
14	Insecurity	Unworthiness
15	Fear	Powerlessness

Energy Barometer

Transformations Institute

© Transformationsinstitute.com

Chapter 10
Step 3: Act
Act Congruently with Your Desires

This is the DOING part. "Finally," I can hear you saying. I know, I hear you, we're a DOING society! We are ingrained in doing, doing, doing. Unfortunately, that's how many people measure their worth - by what they do. That is so WRONG!

In this model, **your DOING comes from your BEING**. If you are BEING healthy, then you do things that are healthy; the things that health conscious individuals do each day. If you are BEING abundant, then you do things that create abundance; get ideas of what to do by finding out what people that are abundant, do. If you are BEING a person seeking a fulfilling job, then you do what it takes to attract that perfect job, such as, create an effective resume, practice interviewing, make contacts, etc. Your DOING is established from your BEING when you stay in the present moment and take actions that support your intentions.

Congruent Behaviors

Let's take a look at your behaviors. You can't say an affirmation like "I make healthy food choices",

act on Inspiration!

then eat a dozen cookies a day and expect to get good results. Your actions must be congruent with your BEING. People also fail when they start with action, which are the behaviors, without becoming clear about their BEING, values, affirmations, and visualization or script. Those things provide the foundation for the acting.

I've noticed that my clients sometimes avoid doing things they would really enjoy because they are worried about what others might think. One woman from a workshop told me that she wanted to dance at a party the weekend before but she didn't because she thought people would say "look at that fat woman out there." This woman only was about ten pounds overweight! Yikes! Do what you want to do, even if you hear that small critical voice in your head telling you not to; **DO IT NOW!**

Once you bring yourself into alignment with your BEING, you can create the essence of what you want now. Nothing has to change on the outside, but with your new BEING, supported by your affirmations and visualization, you can dance, ride a bike, wear fashionable clothes that fit, or just smile and laugh, NOW! Once you give up caring about what others think about what you DO, what they'll actually notice is you BEING WOW and they'll want what you have.

What is WOW? WOW is feeling terrific! Leading a healthy vibrant life, with enough energy to do all the things you want to do. WOW is feeling proud of how you look, regardless of your size. Accepting compliments, complimenting yourself, feeling attractive, sexy and comfortable in clothes that are stylish and fit perfectly! WOW is being mentally nourished, loving yourself completely and feeling positive, upbeat and happy. It's peace of mind knowing you are the perfect role model for those that look up to you. WOW is being in the moment, knowing that in every second you have the power of choice. To choose health, love or abundance; to actually choose to DO the things you want to do; to take actions that are based on the BEING you've chosen.

You can have WOW right now; it's just a choice you make to act congruently with your intentions. Be WOW, right now, by taking inspired actions that lead you to the end result you desire.

Take Inspired Actions

Your job is to clarify your intention, align yourself and your vibration with what you want, and then let the Universe take care of the HOW. You watch for opportunities to come along and determine if they are right for you. Become a good listener - listen to what your intuition tells you and follow that guidance, taking the action steps that are revealed to you. For example, a friend may call you about a massage therapist that she's just tried and your quiet voice within urges you to schedule a massage for yourself. When you hear those urgings, "Just Do It" as the famous shoe commercial says.

Your intuition may speak to you in a variety of ways, through feelings, dreams, the inner voice, body signals, someone else suggesting something that you've also been considering, etc. When you stay in the NOW and in positive vibration, you are more able to hear your intuition speaking.

Lynn Robinson, author of many interesting books on intuition, including my favorite, *Divine Intuition*, says, "Developing intuition is like learning to develop any skill, whether it be mastering a new computer software program or becoming proficient at a musical instrument. That is, the more you use your intuition the better you get at it."

Lynn believes intuition becomes second nature when you practice it. If you use intuition regularly you will develop an "instant knowing." The sixth sense, the hunch, the gut feeling becomes a sure thing and can be trusted and relied upon when pursuing a life change, such as releasing a perfectionist mindset or making an important decision.

This is important because if you are present and aware of your intuition, the perfect "doing" actions, that are aligned with you, will just unfold, step by step. For example, let's say that you intend to release the instant gratification mindset and believe that incorporating stress management techniques would make staying conscious and in the moment easier. There are a variety of things you could do, such as:

➤ **Exercise regularly;** schedule exercise into your planner to make sure you fit it in.

➤ **Protect your time;** commit to only those things you know you are going to enjoy, release current commitments that don't energize you.

➤ **Relax daily;** meditate, listen to a guided imagery CD, have a massage.

➤ **Clean your clutter;** commit to throwing out or giving away one item per day.

➤ **Wind down with music and calming scents;** combine meditative musical rhythms or classical music with some lavender oil on your pulse points.

Your task is to quiet your mind, take a few deep breaths and ask yourself "What actions, within this new behavior of stress management, are best for me?" An answer will be presented to you, it might not be immediately, but you will hear from your intuition! Then take that action.

My clients always ask me "How do I know if it's my intuition or just me making something up?" You will know because your intuition always has your best interests at heart. Following your intuition will energize you, lift your spirits and create a high vibration. Your intuition will never lead you astray; it's not judgmental, harsh nor critical. Your intuition is unemotional.

I rely on my intuition for both big and small decisions in my life. I have even found it helpful when trying to find lost items! My intuition sounds just like me, but I know it's not me. Here's why: I returned home on a Sunday evening from one of the semi-annual retreats that I deliver. My husband, sweet guy that he is, greeted me and then unloaded the car and even unpacked my suitcase. On Monday, I couldn't find my favorite black slide boots (the slip on kind with no back; do you know the type? You can wear them with everything, everyday). Those boots – missing! I decided to quiet my mind and ask my intuition where the boots were. Immediately, I heard, "In the closet." So I went into my closet and looked through the disarray of shoes on the floor but no boots, so I wore my back up black shoes. On Tuesday, I asked again and immediately heard "In the closet." Instead of just looking through the mess of shoes, I actually cleaned them up; WOW, a nice tidy closet floor with shoes lined up in pairs but NO black slide boots. I also checked with the retreat center and my driving partner and neither had seen my boots.

On Wednesday, while driving home from an out-of-town presentation I thought maybe I was putting too much low energy vibration out (NOT having my boots) and so I decided to reframe my thoughts into positive vibration. So I began by remembering how much I loved to wear those boots, how comfortable they are, and on and on! Then I asked my intuition again where the shoes were and I heard "In the closet." "No way, I've been through the closet" was my reply, but when I got home I thought I'd go into the closet one more time and again, the shoes were not on the floor. When I turned to leave the closet, I noticed, hanging on a hook in the closet (right where my husband put it for me to unpack), was a small garment bag that I used to carry a pair of trousers up to the retreat center. There was a bulge in the bottom of the bag and sure enough, there were my boots, in the closet the entire time!

The morale of the story is if this had been me talking to myself, by the third time of asking the same question, I would have been screaming back in a loud voice "I ALREADY TOLD YOU – THEY ARE IN THE CLOSET!" or "COULD YOU ASK A DIFFERENT

QUESTION, I'VE ALREADY ANSWERED THAT ONE!" My voice, while it sounds the same as the voice of my intuition, is nothing like the unemotional "In the closet" response I kept hearing.

If you still aren't sure which actions to select after listening for your intuition, just choose one and start with that. Over time you'll know if it feels right to you. If it does, continue with that action. Let's say that as part of your stress management practices, you decide to take a yoga class. Once you are involved in the class, you will know if it uplifts you or if it's draining to you, so you can assess whether to make it a permanent part of your routine or not. Continue with activities that elevate your vibration because those will always be the actions that are right for you.

Summary

This chapter described one part of the DO step in the BE-DO-HAVE model. Your DOING must be congruent with the BEING you've selected and when it is, you ignite your inner power! You can achieve what you want because your actions are in alignment with your intentions. In the next chapter, we'll talk about a method for easily keeping yourself accountable for changes you are making in your behaviors and actions. You will also find out more about DOING in Chapter 13, Nurture Your Energy.

Chapter 11
Step 4: Account
Account for Your Actions

Tracking your actions as you make behavior changes helps you stay accountable. For example, if you decide to meditate daily, it's easy to say, "I'll remember to do that everyday" and then when you don't do it, you think "I'll start tomorrow." But, tomorrow never comes, UNLESS you commit to your new behavior is and implement a tracking system. This chapter will show you how to follow through on your intentions by engaging persistence and accountability.

Persistence

Persistence is defined as "continuing in spite of opposition or difficulty" or "continually doing what it takes." A favorite framed quote that I keep on my desk says "Persistence prevails when all else fails." People start and then give up. We tend to throw our goals and intentions overboard at the first signs of white caps! You no longer need to do that; there is a way that feels more like smooth sailing.

The easiest way to engage persistence is to align yourself daily with what you want. Every day take the

actions in Step 2 - Align – do this EVERYDAY! How hard can that be? You get to spend some time each day visualizing and passionately feeling the emotions of having what you desire. Yet, people resist. Why? They say "I don't have time to do it every day" or "I got really busy and forgot."

A subconscious core belief that hasn't been discovered and released frequently is the cause of their inability to do what it takes. If this is happening to you, go back over the mindset chapters and use Appendix A to release any limiting core beliefs that might be holding you back from achieving your dreams.

Winston Churchill said:

"Never, never, never give up!"

Keep your dreams alive by spending time each morning and evening cultivating a deep desire; become genuinely passionate about achieving your intentions. Visualize the essence of what you desire as if it has already shown up in your life. Throughout the day, associate with people who support you and are excited to encourage your passion. Doing this will help you maintain persistence when you get stuck.

Here's what I found from working with my clients, and in my own life too, when you choose success and make a decision to implement new strategies invariably something happens to throw you off course. It could be that someone you respect implies that you can't achieve what you want, you may find that you can't motivate yourself to take the actions you have selected or heavin forbid, you don't get the immediate results you were hoping for. Then what happens? Typically you stop dead in your tracks - I call this coming face to face with the brick wall.

It's your point of choice. The cool thing about the point of choice is that you can recognize it by your behaviors, or lack thereof, and the feelings you have, which for the most part, are fear related. Once you wake up and become conscious of the fact that you are facing a brick wall, you can activate your power of choice. Then decide what alignment strategies to take to neutralize your fears and refocus on the actions you have chosen to take.

To do that, first get yourself relaxed, in whatever way that works for you. Then do a few stretches. I like stretches that cross over the body, such as toe touches. Touch your left toe with your right hand and your right toe with your left hand. Believe it or not, moving in this way, helps to center and balance you and connect both parts of your brain - the analytical and the emotional.

Once you are relaxed and feeling balanced, start asking yourself "Why" questions: Why can't I make the calls? Why can't I motivate myself to exercise? Why can't I choose the apple instead of the candy bar? Why can't I believe in myself? Ask the questions that are pertinent to your situation.

Some people like to journal while they are answering their questions. Keep asking and answering until you begin to see the nature of the fear represented by the brick wall. By bringing it to light, it loses it's power over you. You may discover a limiting belief to release using the Transformations

Breakthrough Process™ in Appendix A. Celebrate your brick wall incidences because they are an opportunity for you to grow and learn more about yourself.

However, it takes self-control to maintain the mindfulness to recognize that you are at the brick wall and to do the analysis required of the "why" questions. So if you don't feel like doing it immediately, don't get down on yourself. Sometimes when we are in the middle of a situation, it's not the right time to analyze it for purposes of expansion. I mention this because researchers have found that self-control energy is a depleting resource. Once you use it to resist something or force yourself to do a certain activity, you have less self-control for the next thing.

For example, researchers tempted a group of participants with warm, freshly baked chocolate chip cookies placed in front of them. They were told they couldn't eat them. After some minutes had passed the researchers brought in another group of people as well as bowls of ice water for each individual. The people who had experienced resisting the cookies could not hold their hands in the ice water for as many minutes as the people who were "fresh."

Depending on the circumstance that causes you to "hit the wall," giving yourself some time to get perspective might be the best option. BUT don't give up on yourself. If you don't ultimately activate your power of choice and use the brick wall for personal growth, eventually you will get unstuck. But instead of moving around the wall, to success, you just drift slowly back to where you started. I believe this is your comfort zone, that all too familiar place complete with all of your old habits and beliefs.

When you activate your power of choice at the brick wall and begin to get into action again, you'll discover that it was simply a challenge to be overcome and once you do, you'll build confidence in your ability to meet other challenges as well. Before you know it, you'll have integrated your new way of BEING into your life!

Accountability

Without some systematic method of daily tracking, it's easy to stray off course. Regardless of your intention, if you have no accountability system, then either old habits or laziness will dictate your life in the end. A daily tracking system, will allow you to look back on your day and notice where you fell short and where you were successful. View it as a record of your success and celebrate yourself for completing the actions you intended. You may even decide to implement a reward system along with the tracking sheet.

If you didn't complete the actions you intended for the day, you can immediately get back on track and recommit to the activity for the next day. It is more effective to do this every evening. Keeping track in your mind is no different than what you do now, right? You think about it for a few days and then it slips away. Ultimately you'll discover a few months from now that you are no closer to your goals and intentions than you were today.

The accountability system I recommend involves self-monitoring each evening using a chart like the one at the end of this chapter. You can also download a master of this from my website at: www.choosesuccessbook.com/Resources.html

Select three to four new actions, congruent with the BEING you've decided upon, that you want to implement. When in the process of changing to a new way of BEING, attempting to incorporate too many new behaviors can be overwhelming. My most successful clients just work with three to four new actions at a time.

For example, let's say in Step 1 – ANNOUNCE, you decide to BE abundant; four action steps you might take, stated from your point of view, are:

1. At 6:30 am each morning do a ten minute visualization of my abundant life.

2. Right before bed each evening write three items I'm thankful for in a gratitude journal.

3. Read one chapter daily in an investing book, starting with *Rich Dad, Poor Dad*.

4. Have 10% of my check or business income automatically withheld for investment.

Using the tracking sheet, write your first three action steps across the top in the "Strategy" section. At the end of each day, you can checkmark the successful completion of these actions. Number four is a one-time event, so there's no need to track that daily. Just do it!

Be specific; the more specific your action steps are, the easier it will be for you to track your progress. Notice how the first item is to visualize for ten minutes at 6:30am, not just visualize. The second strategy is to write three items in a gratitude journal each evening, before bed, not just write in a journal. Making your action steps measurable and associated with a certain time of day will help you to be more successful. Each evening when you complete your tracking sheet, you can do an action audit. Are you doing what you committed to do? If not, why? Maybe you took on too much or maybe you need to find what's blocking you from doing what you say you want to do. The nightly accountability is an opportunity to tweak and make changes that fit your life, rather than going on auto pilot without even realizing you aren't doing enough to accomplish your goal.

Consistency is important when implementing new behaviors; daily tracking in this manner will improve your odds of success. Stop tracking the new behavior when it becomes a tradition in your life, just like brushing your teeth or showering. Using our earlier example, once you know that you will always start each day with a ten minute visualization because you recognize the impact it's had on your life, you can select a new behavior to implement and remove the visualization from your tracking sheet.

Janette told me she hated exercise. She had some physical issues which made it uncomfortable for her to move her body; however, she understood that if she made the effort to move, her issues would most likely ease up. With that in mind, Janette decided to hold herself accountable for ten minutes of stretching each morning at 7am. As she gradually incorporated the morning stretch as a tradition and tracked it each day, Janette noticed that she had more energy and felt better physcially on the days that she stretched. Stretching no longer was a strategy on her tracking sheet once she had that realization and commited to herself to make ten minutes of stretching part of her daily regimen. She then found a new strategy to add to her tracking sheet.

In fact, Janette began to open herself up to more types of movement. Her friends asked her to join a Zumba class, so she did and loved it. Then they encouraged her to take kick boxing. Last I heard, Janette had enrolled in a running camp. This all happened within six months of her beginning to track a ten minute stretch as a new behavior.

Summary

Accountability is making a commitment to take action and then following through to make sure that you do it by using a tracking system. It is not an inborn quality, but is one that you can develop with practice. Get started today to improve your accountability by tracking the new congruent behaviors you'd like to implement.

Daily Accountability Tracking Sheet

Days:	Strategies:			
1				
2				
3				
4				
5				
6				
7				
8				
9				
10				
11				
12				
13				
14				
15				
16				
17				
18				
19				
20				
21				

Instructions:
Write a description for at least 3 strategies you plan to implement in the strategy section
Each day for the next three weeks put a check mark when you execute that strategy

Transformations Institute

Chapter 12
Step 5: Allow
Allow What You Want Into Your Life

It's time now to HAVE. You can attract what you desire when you decide to be certain. Allowing is the absence of doubt. Whenever you catch yourself doubting or fearing, stop those thoughts in their tracks, do not let them progress, but do not resist them because that which you resist, persists. When you resist something, you generate lower vibration thoughts and feelings. Then what do you create in your life? Exactly, more of those types of thoughts and situations along with difficulty motivating yourself to take action! Instead just mindfully notice them, see where they come from, why and how long they last. You may even want to write about the thoughts and emotions you experience in your journal. Then you can use that information to help release the beliefs that are behind them.

Believe

Jesus said:

"Everything is possible for him who believes."

When you pick up a toothbrush to brush your teeth, you know without a shred of doubt that you will not fail to pick it up. The thought that you may not be able to pick up the toothbrush never even occurs to you. You do it with certainty. That is the level of conviction and certainty you should have in yourself, the Laws of the Universe, and the capabilities of the Divine to work perfectly every time. After all, you have received even before you asked; that's the promise.

People who continuously worry about things are thinking and talking themselves into doubt. That doubt prevents them from manifesting what they desire. You truly do light up your desire when you have absolute faith that it will manifest into physical reality. With faith, you can take actions without anxiety, which assures you of an ultimate satisfactory result.

Faith comes from believing something is possible. Even things you fear are alive with your faith - what if I lose my job? My house? My spouse? - you fear these things because you think they are possible.

Most of us have been programmed to fear failure. We give up too soon to avoid it. Sometimes, we do not even attempt something just to steer clear of a potential failure. Have you ever done that? Yo-yo dieters know the feeling. After failing at so many diets, after so many times of telling their family and friends with great anticipation that they are going on a diet, after feeling like a total loser because they couldn't stick to some fad diet, they get leery of trying again and failing yet one more time. Failure is viewed by our society as something shocking or appalling when in effect it really is purely a learning experience. It helps correct wrong thoughts. So don't give up!

Worry and fear creates upsetting images in your mind and attracts more low vibration feelings and most likely, exactly what you are worried about! Can you think of a time when you did that? Remember Pam from the "What is Your Mindset Telling You" chapter; her fear was that she would be rejected and abandoned. Of course, she proceeded to attract a man that had an affair while married to her.

The best way to heal fear and worry is to face it. Analyze it fully, break it down into its components, look for the limiting core beliefs and see where the false evidence lies. Psychologist and author, Dr. Wayne Dyer says that FEAR is an acronym for False Evidence Appearing Real! How true; there is always false evidence behind our fears.

If you want something but then block it with inner conflicts, fears, and lack of faith, what will you manifest? Certainly not what you want! You have stated and clarified your intention and are aligning with it; however, if you don't have faith, your habits of thought are contradictory or limiting. Basically, you won't allow your intention to manifest.

Take Annie, a beautiful woman, who owns her own business as a financial planner and has everything necessary to be successful and happy, including a really fun sense of humor and great family. But, when I first met her, she was extremely unhappy and about 40 pounds overweight. It turns out all her life she'd been called flighty by her mother and in fact, when she started her business, her mom told her she'd have to be professional and serious if she had any hope of succeeding. So Annie started using her formal name, Anna, and became a more serious person watching every word she said because she was afraid she might slip up and say something humorous, which she figured might come across as inappropriate or would shock her clients! It took a lot of effort to keep her real self buried and eating was her escape. So her lack of faith came because she wanted to lose the weight and have a successful business but deep inside her belief was that she wasn't capable of that because she was flighty and inappropriately funny!

That's called having door issues. Annie was opening the door of possibility with her positive vibration around the intention of losing weight and building her business, but was pushing the close button on the door with her limiting belief which was "I am not capable….." She had a stong desire to be successful and was doing affirmations and visualization but she also had a limiting core belief which blocked the receipt of what she wanted due to lack of faith. This same thing happens to so many people if they don't realize to look for their own "door issue." Instead, they give up and say they don't have enough will power to change, that manifesting doesn't work or whatever other reason they have for giving up.

Uncovering limiting beliefs, like Annie's belief that she wasn't capable, and stepping into the BEING of what you want to manifest, with faith that it will manifest, is the key to permanent change. Most core beliefs are so ingrained in our subconscious that we merely think FROM them and not about them. Being aware and noticing your door issues will help you uncover your limiting beliefs, which you can then release using the Transformations Breakthrough Process™ in Appendix A.

Once you have released your limiting beliefs, then create faith, if you don't have it now, by looking for examples of other people who have what you want. If they have the outcome you desire, you can too! Just remember that you are as powerful as you decide to be, so go for it with persistence!

Detachment

Just like the Universe takes care of the HOW, it also takes care of the WHEN. When you are detached, you enjoy the NOW and stay in the belief that your intention will manifest. Don't think about the past and project it into the future, just focus on your desires. If you have low energy, use the Emotion Perception Scale, on page 101, to work your way back up into positive vibration.

Detachment means to live this moment to the fullest with the highest vibration you can create.

When you plant a seed in your garden, you know your creation is underway, silently happening under the ground, before you see any physical evidence. It's highly unlikely that you'd go out and stomp on the ground, demanding to see physical evidence of the seed maturing! You don't pull it up to see where it is in the growth stage. Instead you allow the natural laws of the Universe to do their work and the small seed matures into what you desire. That is detachment and belief in action! Release expectations that changes in your life will manifest within a certain period of time. Once you do, you'll be practicing the principle of detachment.

Mandy was a participant in one of my Clarify and Attract Your Perfect Customer courses; along with attracting perfect clients, Mandy was also interested in attracting a relationship. She completed the Contrast Brings Clearness form and had a thorough description of her perfect life partner. At one of our classroom breaks, Mandy approached me and wanted to know how long until she would hear from this certain man. "What man?" I inquired. It turns out that Mandy thought by completing the Contrast Brings Clearness form she could attract this certain person that she wanted to date. I'm sorry, but it doesn't work that way! That is being attached to the outcome and when you are attached in that way, you miss out on all sorts of other, possibly better opportunities, clients, relationships, etc., whatever you are hoping to manifest.

Don't set yourself up for frustration by being attached to the result happening a certain way or on your time frame.

Gratitude

Gratitude creates an especially high vibration. Practicing gratitude every day is a very powerful. Be grateful for what you are trying to manifest, as if it were in your life NOW; this process helps attract it to you!

Roberta and her husband decided they wanted to manifest financial abundance. Together, they completed a Contrast Brings Clearness™ worksheet to clarify their intention and developed affirmations to reach their goal. They made sure to include the word "joyful" in their affirmations as a daily reminder to stay focused on the fun involved in their journey.

Within a three-week period, they were thrilled to realize that money was starting to roll in from a variety of unanticipated sources. The landlord for Roberta's late father's estate agreed to waive the rent for a few months – a financial windfall of $600! Roberta's husband received a check for $75 from a former student who'd taken a martial arts class last year but failed to pay due to financial hardship. Roberta also received a long overdue payment from the parent of one of her day-care students. And new students – for both Roberta and her husband – began appearing in droves. Roberta's son even volunteered to pay for her recent birthday dinner at a favorite restaurant – something he's never done before.

Roberta noticed the key for her is recognizing and being grateful for the small ways abundance is arriving in her life. In doing so, she noted, the Laws of the Universe seem to be bringing even more prosperity to her family.

Really take the time to appreciate all the wonderful, terrific things in your life...no matter how small they are...simple things like the beauty of nature, a blue sky, the beach, a great meal, good friends, a kind act, your job.

Here's a gratefulness process that I recommend:

1. **Morning** - appreciate the new day and all the opportunities you have that day to BE who you are.

2. **Lunch** – be grateful for what hasn't arrived yet as if you already have it, visualize how appreciative you are.

3. **Dinner** – appreciate all the people in your life, the wonderful ones and even those that you struggle to enjoy.

4. **End of day** – appreciate everything that happened that day; the lessons you learned and the FUN you had.

It's not necessary to write these down, just get in the habit of thinking about what you are grateful for throughout the day, there's no better way to acknowledge the blessings in your life.

Summary

This completes the chapters covering the Conscious Transformation Process™. Using this easy step-by-step process of: Announce, Align, Act, Account, and Allow, in conjunction with aligned core beliefs and mindsets, you will BE successful and attract everything that you desire in the area of relationships, career, health, business or finances.

Summary of the Conscious Transformation Process™:

1. **ANNOUNCE** what you want clearly.

2. **ALIGN** yourself and your vibration with your intention.

3. **ACT** upon inspiration and congruent to your intention.

4. **ACCOUNT** and keep track of your new action steps.

5. **ALLOW** your intention to arrive by clearing any vibrations that contradict your goal.

Energy Management

Chapter 13
Nurture Your Energy

Transforming your life always requires change and who likes that? Not many of us. However, while you are implementing the Conscious Transformation Process™ to attract what you desire, if you manage your energy and nurture yourself, you will have the strength to make needed changes.

Alcoholic, anorexic and alone, 47 year old sober Jeanne showed up in my office feeling scared and desperate. Emotionally and physically abused by her family, who had struggled for ten years to cope with her behavior without reaching out for help for themselves, Jeanne knew it was time to make permanent changes before it was too late. Too late to save her life!

Jeanne is also attractive, smart, and employed as a consultant (just shy of receiving a PhD). She has a therapist and occasionally attends AA; however, she provided me with excuses for not being a regular participant in that program. So why did she need me? One word – **energy!** No one ever explained to her that the abuse she was putting her physical body through was affecting her mental, emotional and spiritual energies to the extent that she couldn't put herself into action to make even simple changes in her lifestyle.

Have you ever noticed that some people seem to be able to adapt to the ebb and flow of life without it affecting their mental and emotional capabilities or outlook? It doesn't seem to matter what it is, any change, such as, a downturn in the economy, the loss of a relationship, or a change in abundance level is just simply viewed as a new challenge or opportunity for learning. Whereas other people, like Jeanne, are thrown for a loop at the least little problem they have to face. Why? I believe it has to do with how well they nurture themselves both physically and spiritually.

I don't know about you, but I didn't grow up knowing how to nurture myself. However, as an adult, once I chose to love myself, I began to implement practices of nurturing that support my mental/emotional dimension. As my physical and spiritual aspects became stronger, I noticed my ability to attract from my inner power as well as expand and grow with challenges, increased.

Jeanne, on the other hand, has been abusing herself physically for 30 years! She became anorexic in her late teens and since then has never nourished her physical body properly. She's actually one of the lucky ones afflicted with this disease for so many years, since she has no signs of permanent damage yet. However, she never had the energy resources to truly love and accept herself since her limited reserves were used to keep her body functioning. The practices she put into place in her life wasted and used her energy in the wrong ways.

As I mentioned in an earlier chapter, researchers have discovered that our conscious capacity for self-control is limited and easily depleted. Every demand that Jeanne makes on her self-control, such as, avoiding alcohol, eating healthy portions, nurturing her body, all draw on the same easily depleted reservoir of energy. Willpower uses this energy whereas traditions conserve it. That's why I encourage you to only adopt three to four new strategies at a time and work with them until they become traditions, thereby, conserving your self-control reserves throughout all dimensions.

Our physical, mental/emotional and spiritual dimensions are all interrelated; however, the physical and spiritual aspects both affect, in differing ways, our ability to maintain high vibration emotions and sharp mental capacity. You can see this portrayed in the **Dimensions of Well-Being** model found at the end of this chapter. Our physical energy flows over to support us mentally and emotionally, while our spiritual energy provides the foundation and supports our other dimensions.

Let's examine this further:

Physical – without adequate physical energy, we have greater difficulty focusing mentally or maintaining our emotional control. When we properly nourish our physical body, we feel energetic, ready to handle any challenge, and are more resilient and optimistic.

How well are you nurturing your physical self?

Are you getting an adequate amount of sleep?

Are you nourishing your body with natural, whole foods?

Are you experiencing daily exercise?

Are you drinking an adequate amount of water?

Are you managing your stress?

When you take excellent care of yourself physically, you have the capacity to handle mental and emotional requirments more easily. Nurturing your physical dimension also gives you the motivation to be interested in nurturing your mental and emotional needs.

Once Jeanne started eating a protein based breakfast, she found that it became easier for her to stay emotionally balanced or at least get herself back into alignment sooner. Jeanne also started saying her affirmations while walking on a treadmill and found that this practice made her feel powerful, energetic and resilient – something she hadn't felt for years. This combination of new daily traditions became the crux of Jeanne's transformation of energy. She became aware of how to utilize her energy for her well being.

Spiritual – without spiritual nurturing, our feelings seem dulled, we have difficulty getting excited about mental challenges, and frequently ask "is this all there is to life?" In contrast, when we give adequate care to our spiritual side, we feel a sense of purpose, a connection to something greater than ourselves, and find that living a life based on our values, helps us to create the changes necessary to grow and expand. Spiritual energy truly is the most powerful source of motivation, perseverance and direction. Without spiritual energy, it's extremely difficult to make changes in your behaviors. How would you answer these questions?

> **When was the last time you took the time to do something that brings you JOY?**
>
> **Are your decisions based on your values?**
>
> **Do you feel connected to a sense of purpose?**
>
> **Do you take time daily to relax completely and reflect, with meditation, guided imagery, journal writing, etc.?**
>
> **Are you grateful for everything in your life - even the challenges that bring you wonderful growing opportunities?**

When you nurture yourself spiritually, you can't help but raise your emotional vibration and increase your mental clarity. Your spiritual energy gives you the ability to maintain a sense of belief in yourself and your dreams and helps you to take the actions necessary to achieve them.

Joy? Jeanne couldn't remember the last time that she did something that brought her joy; in fact, she couldn't even think of one thing that she could do to feel joyful. With just a little prompting to think way back to before the alcohol problems took hold, she managed to come up with some ideas and slowly started opening herself up to begin doing those things again. Jeanne, like many anorexics, has strong perfectionist tendencies, so it was important for her to choose to do things that couldn't be evaluated. Some of her ideas included walking her dog in the woods, reading a book by the fire, writing in a journal, attending her favorite country Church. These then ultimately led to other things such as, sewing, creating a beautiful environment to reside in, and thoroughly becoming immersed in her work.

If you aren't nurturing yourself physically and spiritually, you might want to begin with the ideas in this chapter and then, when you feel balanced, return to "choosing success." Start by **incorporating one new behavior** in each dimension and hold yourself accountable for doing it using the Daily Accountability Tracking Sheet from Chapter 11.

For example, you might decide 1) physical - drink 48 ounces of water each day and 2) spiritual - start your day with 15 minutes of meditation. Each evening, before going to bed, complete your action audit to access your day. If you did not incorporate the new behaviors, look within to find out why not. Perhaps you were too aggressive with your new commitments or maybe there's something within that needs to be cleared; something that's blocking you from nurturing yourself. If you did complete the new activities, give yourself a pat on the back.

Summary

Once you begin to consciously nurture your energy, you'll find it easier and easier to incorporate new supportive behaviors into your life. You'll have the motivation to take the actions necessary to achieve your goals. In addition, anything you do for yourself will have a ripple effect on those around you.

Once you begin to nurture yourself, you'll become a role model for others! Wouldn't it be wonderful if children grew up knowing how to BE healthy physically and connected spiritually? You can help your children and grandchildren; heck, the entire planet, just by starting with yourself. Like they say on the airplane with the oxygen mask, take care of yourself first and then you can help others.

Dimensions of Well-Being

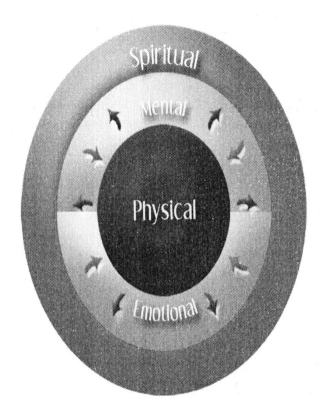

Spiritual

Mental

Physical

Emotional

Transformations
Institute

Chapter 14
Align & Soar

Attracting from your inner power happens when you manage your energy as you align your core beliefs, mindsets, thoughts, emotions and actions. If you are not in alignment, it doesn't matter how hard you work at attracting success, a perfect relationship, financial wealth, a healthy body or anything else you want, your inner power WILL NOT be ignited. This misalignment causes confusion and a vibration that may actually attract what you DON'T want!

Kathy always wanted a business of her own. Throughout her successful career working for others, she always had some sort of side business, but none of her endeavors ever created enough income to leave the safety of the corporate environment. Upon attending a Conscious Transformation Process™ workshop of mine, Kathy immediately completed the Contrast Brings Clearness™ form and started repeating the following affirmation *"I am a successful entrepreneur."* She attended seminars on how to start a business and set up her bookkeeping and marketing systems properly. Kathy seemed to be on the right track, but the success she desired eluded her. "This

manifesting doesn't work!" was what she said to me in utter frustration after following the steps of the Conscious Transformation Process™ precisely.

Can you guess Kathy's mindset? Right! She's a perfectionist. After just two coaching sessions, Kathy realized that her perfectionist mindset and limiting core belief of "I'm not capable" were holding her back from completing important tasks that could lead to her success. Her emotion of FEAR, diminished her faith. The good news is that once she released her fears, she was able to leave her corporate position within three months and is now a successful entrepreneur.

To ignite your inner power and choose success, align your mindset and core beliefs with your desires, just like Kathy. Use your feelings and thoughts to uncover limiting beliefs that may be holding you back, then release them using the Transformations Breakthrough Process™ found in Appendix A. Keep your energy and faith high and strong by nurturing yourself physically and spiritually.

You've probably heard the peeling of the onion analogy; that's exactly what the process of uncovering and releasing limiting beliefs and mindsets is like. Everyone has these limitations to some extent and not just one, so don't feel bad! It's a fun process of self-discovery and with each step to new awareness, you ignite your inner power more.

I wish you success and happiness and don't forget, you can have the essence of what you want, right NOW! Just BE it! I'd love to hear your stories so please feel free to contact me anytime at pat@ transformationsinstitute.com.

Appendices

Appendix A
Transformations Breakthrough Process™

    The following pages outline the Transformations Breakthrough Process™ for releasing limiting beliefs, that I developed working one-on-one with clients. I strongly recommend that you use this technique with a trusted friend as a support person in lieu of having a coach to help you through the process.

    We are usually our own worst critic. Amazing, isn't it? How about if we replace our inner critic with a cheering fan that applauds, encourages and comforts us. I've got mine; do you have yours? Take a minute and visualize your mental cheering fan. This is a part of you and is always there to applaud your personal growth efforts.

    Thinking about limiting beliefs brings out many people's inner critic with thoughts that reinforce the limiting belief; thoughts like "I'm not capable of changing" or "I'm not worthy, good enough, or deserving of this." Those are the very beliefs you may be trying to release and so it helps to have an independent support person available to remind you that anything is possible and you can change.

As you work through the process on the next few pages, connect to the feelings associated with the consequences you've experienced or will experience in your life as a result of holding the limiting belief. Then, once you've replaced the old belief with a new one, ask yourself how holding the new belief makes you feel. Are you joyful, excited, inspired and truly optimistic? Most people feel a huge shift in their energy. This surge of high vibration emotion affects your ability to get into action and you'll begin to witness all the wonderful benefits of holding this new belief.

Get started now. Be gentle with yourself, invite in your cheering fan and use the Transformations Breakthrough Process™ with positive expectancy. Remember, we are all human; no one is perfect!

Transformations Breakthrough Process Step 1: Awareness

The purpose of this step is to uncover limiting beliefs that may be keeping you from achieving your desires. Doubt is one indication that you may be sabotaging yourself, so write down any doubts you have about achieving your intentions. If you have difficulty with this, try to answer the question "I can't achieve this because...."

_____

_____

_____

_____

Since thoughts come from beliefs, even if the belief is unconscious, analyzing your thoughts can help you uncover the belief. Ask yourself the questions below to go deeper into your thoughts to understand the who, what, where, when and why of the thought until you finally get to the belief. Ask the questions, in the order that feels right to you and record your thoughts in the column on the left below or in your journal. **If you already know your limiting belief, go to the next page and Step 2.**

Your Thoughts:

_____

_____

_____

_____

_____

_____

_____

_____

_____

_____

Possible questions to ask yourself:

What do I really want?

Why would that cause me to feel _____?

What is the impact I want? Why?

What aren't I admitting?

What more is there to this?

What else?

What is important about that?

How do I want to be?

What does this mean?

How can I use this information?

Transformations Breakthrough Process
Step 2: Acceptance

Change requires acceptance! Accept yourself as a human being with WORTH! Learn to rate only your behavior and not your worth. Know that you can be happy any time you choose to be, so why not NOW!

Based on your analysis in Step 1, what is your limiting belief?

_____

_____

Is the belief valid? What evidence in your life proves the belief is not valid?

_____

_____

_____

_____

Further analyze how your limited behavior is affecting you.

This limiting belief shows up in my behavior when I:

_____

_____

How has this behavior hurt me in the past?

_____

_____

_____

_____

What are the consequences of continuing this type of behavior?

_____

_____

_____

_____

_____

Decide if you are ready to let go of this belief.

Is it to my advantage to hang on to this belief? What am I achieving by keeping it?

_____

_____

Do I want to let it go NOW? _____
In what way will my life be different?

_____

_____

Transformations Breakthrough Process
Step 3: Adjustment

You have the power within you to change! Are you ready?

Symbolically release the old belief, using a technique that works for you (See Appendix B for some of my favorite ways). What technique will you use?

_____

Now that you symbolically released the old belief, what new belief are you adopting to re-place it?

_____

_____

_____

How excited are you to have this new belief?

_____

Use the Conscious Transformation Process™ to focus on your new belief.

Step 1 - Announce. *What are the traits you want:*

_____

_____

_____

_____

Step 2 - Align. *How will you concentrate on your intention?*

_____

_____

_____

_____

_____

Step 3 & 4- Act & Account. *What new behaviors will you adopt? How will you be accountable?*

_____

_____

_____

_____

Step 5 - Allow. *How will you BE the new belief and detach and express gratitude? How do you feel emotionally now?*

_____

_____

_____

_____

Note: Reread Chapters 8-12 for information about the Conscious Transformation Process™.

Appendix B
Symbolic Methods for Releasing Limiting Beliefs

In the process of releasing limiting beliefs, some people find it helpful to also visualize the belief being released from their body. The following are some of the common visualizations that are used:

1. See a ball of light entering the top of your head and passing through all parts of your body collecting up the remnants of your limiting belief. The ball of light clears each area, absorbing your limiting belief and leaving the area pure and whole. Once collected, see this ball of light:

    a. Leaving your body and going into the earth to be cleansed,

    b. Seeping out of your body and into a large lake or pond for cleansing, or

    c. Being placed on a barge that is moving quickly out of sight.

2. Write your limiting belief on a piece of paper:

    a. Affirm that you are no longer going to behave in accordance with the limiting belief, then burn the belief and state your new belief.

   b. After burning the limiting belief, blow the ashes away and watch them dissipate.

3. Release using your breath. Relax yourself and inhale a large breath. Hold the breath for 10 seconds, then forcefully exhale, expelling the limiting belief with the breath.

4. See the belief as a very small symbol in your hand. Perhaps it's a ball and chain or maybe a padlock. Thank it for the lesson you learned from holding that belief and then blow it out of your hand with a strong breath. As it disappears see the symbol dissolve into pure white light.

5. Using your mind, throw the belief into a large fire and watch it disappear into pure energy as it burns.

6. Use an energy technique such as EFT or Psych K to release the belief.

Don't forget to say a thank you prayer to God (using whatever name you please) for the new belief you now hold. Don't mention the old belief. Your prayer can be as simple as "Thank you, God, for this release and my new belief. I am _____ (fill in with your new belief - lovable, worthy, deserving). So it is."

Resources & Suggested Reading

References &
Suggested Reading

Abramson, Edward, Ph.D. *Body Intelligence*
Publisher: McGraw Hill, 2005

Bermont, Debbie *Outrageous Business Growth*
Publisher: Morgan James Publishing, LLC, 2006

Borysenko, Joan *The Power of the Mind to Heal*
Publisher: Hay House, 1995

Braden, Gregg *The Divine Matrix*
Publisher: Hay House, 2008

Braden, Gregg *The Spontaneous Healing of Belief*
Publisher: Hay House, 2009

Burns, David D., Ph.D *The Feeling Good Handbook*
Publisher: Penquin Group, 1990

Canfield, Jack *The Success Principles*
Publisher: HarperCollins Publishers, 2005

Chopra, Deepak *The Seven Spiritual Laws of Success*
Publisher: Amber-Allen Publishing and New World Library, 1994

Covey, Stephen *The 7 Habits of Highly Effective People*
Publisher: Simon Schuster, 1989

Dweck, Carol, Ph.D. *Mindset*
Publisher: Ballantine Books, 2006

Dyer, Dr. Wayne W. *Manifest Your Destiny*
Publisher: HarperPerennial, 1997

Eden, Donna *Energy Medicine*
Publisher: Jeremy P. Tarcher/Putnum 1998

Hanson, Rebecca *Law of Attraction for Business*
Publisher: Rebecca Hanson, 2004

Hay, Louise L. *You Can Heal Your Life*
Publisher: Hay House Inc., 1984

Hicks, Esther and Jerry *Ask and It Is Given*
Publisher: Hay House, Inc., 2004

Jampolsky, Gerald, M.D. *Love is Letting Go of Fear*
Publisher: Celestial Arts, 1979

Kiyosaki, Robert T. *Rich Dad, Poor Dad*
Publisher: Business Plus; 1 edition, 2000

Kohn, Alfie *No Contest*
Publisher: Houghton Miffin Company, 1986

Lipton, Bruce *The Biology of Belief*
Publisher: Hay House, 2008

Loehr, Jim and Tony Schwartz *The Power of Full Engagement*
Publisher: The Free Press, 2003

Losier, Michael J. *Law of Attraction*
Publisher: Michael J. Losier Enterprises, 2006

Luskin, Dr. Fred *Forgive for Good*
Publisher: HarperCollins Publishers, 2002

Pert, Candace *Molecules of Emotion*
Publisher: Simon & Schuster, 1999

Peirce, Penny *frequency*
Publisher: Atria Books, 2009

Robinson, Lynn *Divine Intuition*
Publisher: Dorling Kindersley Publishing Inc.. 2001

Roman, Sanaya & Duane Packer *Creating Money*
Publisher: New World Library, 1988

Schneider, Bruce D., *Energy Leadership*
Publisher: John Wiley and Sons, 2008

Vanzant, Iyanla *In the Meantime: Finding Yourself and the Love you Want*
Publisher: Fireside, 1998

Workshops & Seminars

Workshops & Seminars
with Pat Altvater,
Author, Trainer, Coach

Pat Altvater has natural credibility which inspires her audiences to take action. Her infectious positive "can-do" attitude has helped hundreds of people achieve their highest potential.

In her entertaining, high-energy style, she packs her presentations full of information, tools and worksheets, real life stories and humor – leaving people saying "WOW – I can BE this now!"

During every presentation, Pat lives her mission of "helping others embrace personal growth, positive change and divine connection in a FUN, joyful manner." With more than 20 years delivering training programs, workshops and retreats, Pat consistently receives rave reviews.

Some of *Pat's current programs, based on the information in this book, include:*

Three Steps to Creating a Success Mindset!

Manifest Your Desires - Ignite the Power Within!

Create a Life That Makes Your Heart Sing!

Create Energetic Balance - Nurture Body, Mind and Spirit

Perfectionism: Stop It From Ruining Your Grades

Examples of Pat's other workshops include:

Mamas Don't Let Your Children Grow Up To Be Dieters!

Why Weight? The Power to Succeed is Within You!

Self-Control: Be a Model, a Role Model!

Pat also enjoys presenting **Transform Yourself** weekend retreats that can be customized to meet the requirements of your team or organization.

Here's what one of her retreat attendees had to say: "Please accept my sincere thanks for creating such a powerful and amazing weekend. The retreat truly lived up to its name – I am transformed inside and out. Your thoughtful combination of body/mind/spirit workshops coupled with your positive energy refilled my inner oil lamp and gave me the boost I needed to let my light shine fully once again. I am changed for the better from this experience and can't wait to do it again next year."
- Marci Hannewald.

To book Pat Altvater for your next conference or event, please contact:

Transformations Institute
419-344-6613

Products & Books

Products & Books
by Pat Altvater

Pat's first e-book, **The Secret of Permanent Weight Loss** teaches you how to release weight using the principles of manifesting. When you do, you improve your chances for successfully making important changes, including releasing unwanted weight permanently! Before you know it, you'll be saying "WOW - look at me NOW!" Find out more at:

www.permanentweightlossebook.com

Pat created the innovative **Women Outsmarting Weight**™ system to help people harness the power of their mind to release weight. Using the principles discussed in this book as the foundation for creating change, the program consists of 3 parts:

➤ the Women Outsmarting Weight binder which includes:
  - a workbook,
  - 18 recorded lessons on 6 CDs
  - 3 guided imagery CDs, and
  - 18 affirmation cards,

➤ 18 weeks of daily e-tips, and

> Feel GREAT in 8 support and accountability circles.

Participants are taught to gradually adopt the behaviors of health-conscious people. One new behavior is introduced every two weeks. Participants are given several different strategies for implementing each new behavior and they then adopt the strategies they believe are most beneficial and focus on those strategies for the full two weeks. Behaviors fall within the entire spectrum of a person: body, mind and spirit.

The Women Outsmarting Weight*™ *Quick Start program offers the workbook, the Transformations Trilogy: Body guided imagery CD and 3 of the 18 lessons mentioned above. To request more information about either program visit:

www.outsmartweight.com

There are two products and one program that complement this book. The **Choose Success Quick Start** program includes a CD with three recorded lessons. The lessons are intended to help you balance your physical, mental/emotional and spiritual energies. Pat also created a deck of **Choose Success Oracle Cards.** These cards will help you identify actions to help you manifest the BEING you desire.

Pat also facilitates Conscious Achievers FIT Accountability Circles for individuals who are serious about quickly creating results. These weekly meetings are structured group coaching meetings, much like a mastermind.

www.choosesuccessbook.com

The ***Transformations Trilogy: Body, Mind, and Spirit,*** guided imagery CDs have helped hundreds of people release weight, reduce stress, boost confidence and/or awaken intuition. There are two tracks on each CD, the guided imagery which is followed by a track of positive affirmations. For more information visit:

www.transformationsinstitute.com/products.html